A Summit Salon® Stylist T...

OVER THE TOP™

Best Guest Practices of Top 20 Stylists!

FOURTH EDITION

WRITTEN BY

MICHAEL COLE AND **MARY COLE**

DESIGN & LAYOUT BY
BRIAN CORNELL

ILLUSTRATIONS BY
ROBB MILLER

SUMMIT SALON BUSINESS CENTER | Proven *SYSTEMS*
Proven *RESULTS*

OVER THE TOP
Best Guest Practices of Top 20 Stylists
FOURTH EDITION
A Summit Salon® Stylist Training Course
Written By: Michael Cole & Mary Cole

Copyright 2011, 2012, 2014–2016
by Summit Salon Business Center, LLC
2600 Fernbrook Lane North, Suite 132
Plymouth, MN, 55447 U.S.A.
1.800.718.5949   www.SummitSalon.com

To discover additional Summit Salon materials and programs please visit *www.SummitSalon.com.*

Written By: Michael Cole and Mary Cole
Cover Design and Interior Layout By: Brian I. Cornell
Illustrations By: Robb Miller

ISBN: 978-0-9830964-9-8

Printed in the United States of America

10 9 8 7 6 5
Fourth Edition: April 2015
Second Printing: January 2016
Third Printing: August 2017
Fourth Printing: September 2018
Fifth Printing: July 2019

OVER THE TOP ☆ TABLE OF CONTENTS

ACKNOWLEDGMENTS

Many people are responsible for the creation of this book. Throughout our lives, countless stylists young and old have shared their experiences, wisdom, and life lessons with us. The quality of our work has been profoundly enhanced by what these extraordinary salon professionals have shared. Because of their generosity, our lives have been greatly enriched.

This book is a tribute to these stylists, for their generosity and courage in sharing their salon experiences, many of which were learned through struggle and sacrifice. We wish to express our gratitude for the difference their wisdom has made in our work. The Summit Salon Business Center faculty also deserves a special mention for their continued generosity and pioneering spirit.

Our thirty years of working with salons has been sustained by the hopes and dreams of the stylists who work there. We know that a vast and wonderful potential exists in the hearts, minds, and bodies of every stylist. We value them and believe they are not problems to be solved, but potential to be developed. The sole purpose of this book is to help stylists discover and reveal that potential.

TESTIMONIALS

Michael and Mary Cole's latest book, Over The Top, *provides stylists with the best guest practices that are proven to be successful for any stylist willing to learn and practice the information and processes taught in the book. Easy to read and understand, with great discussion topics that make the information relevant to each stylist,* Over The Top *is undoubtedly the best resource for stylist development on the market today!*

– Pat Parenty, Retired President, L'Oréal Professional Products Division U.S.

In an industry where getting to the top and staying there means that stylists must constantly learn and evolve, Over The Top *has captured the principles and practices that will ensure your journey will be a success. A concise and entertaining way to learn.*

– Glenn Baker, Senior Director of Consulting, Summit Salon Business Center

Over The Top *is a brilliant illustration and road map to the behaviors that separate the few from the many in our industry. It is a must-read for any salon professional looking to grow their income and their life to the next level.*

– Peter Mahoney, President, CEO, Summit Salon Business Center

---

This book speaks to my passion, the anatomy of the intelligent hairdresser! Each chapter provides a fresh perspective and is riddled with best practice after best practice that reaches the heart of our industry, the hairdresser. Michael and Mary have captured the simplest, yet most complex concepts that if followed properly will translate into a prosperous and fulfilling career for a new or seasoned stylist. Thank you for reaching out and creating a platform that not only inspires, but does so in a way that will benefit this generation as well as many generations to come.

– Heather Bagby, Vice President, Business Development, COO, Summit Salon Business Center

I have spent my entire thirty years in the beauty business with Michael and Mary Cole ... as a fan, as an employee, and now as a business partner. Their impact on salon professionals over those years is immeasurable. I believe that Over The Top *will become THE textbook for teaching yet another generation of salon professionals the business side of their craft.*

– Dave Kirby, Senior Director of Education and Training,
   Summit Salon Business Center

Michael and Mary Cole's Over The Top *offers valuable insight on the key building blocks that help salon professionals build the foundation for successful, profitable businesses. Education and passion are the two drivers that steered Redken into holding the number one educational program in the industry; Michael and Mary Cole detail these two principles throughout the book. I strongly encourage every salon stylist to invest in this book.*

– Christine Schuster, Senior VP, Education,
   L'Oréal Professional Products Division U.S.

Over The Top *is a unique learning tool to assist you in becoming a Top 20 Stylist. This amazing 'tool kit' assists you with what it takes to become a successful stylist.* Over The Top *assists The Salon Professional Academy in teaching these skills to our students as we continue in our mission of growing salon leaders one student at a time.*

– Jodi Ellingson and Jill Krahn,
   The Salon Professional Academy, Fargo, ND

Over The Top *is filled with the best practices that hairdressers need in today's world to be successful. Michael and Mary Cole are industry leaders. They understand Self Concept—a combination of SELF IDEAL, (who you want to BE), SELF IMAGE (how you SEE yourself) and SELF-ESTEEM (how much you LOVE yourself). Whether you've lost one of these... or not,* Over The Top *is a must-have.*

– Chris Baran, Artistic Director, Redken 5th Avenue
   NYC Education • President, Fuel Education Systems

When your professional commitment is wavering and you just want to finish that last guest and go home, what can you do? Pick up Over The Top! *Michael and Mary Cole offer insights and techniques for improving job performance and achieving immediate results. I urge you to read and act on this engaging and insightful training course and find out why Michael and Mary Cole continue to bring peace and fulfillment to thousands of hairdressers.*

– Sam Villa, Redken Global Artistic Ambassador,
   Co-founder SAM VILLA / samvilla.com

Over The Top *provides current, relevant principles to support you on your way to the Top 20! Are you ready for prosperity? Hold on ... with* Over The Top, *your dreams become attainable goals and achievement feels oh so good! This book is an incredibly valuable resource supporting our students and graduates on the fastest, smartest path to abundance!*

– Darci Gutfreund, Director, School Division,
   Summit Salon Business Center

WOW! Michael and Mary Cole have gone 'one better' once again. Over The Top—*OVER THE TOP! This book has the benefit of Michael and Mary's wisdom throughout the years. Not just a book with text, it's an illustrative workbook that urges you to take your own notes and write out what's meaningful to you as a stylist. What gets written, gets measured. What gets measured, gets done. What better place to write the goal, the dream, the vision, than right on the pages where Michael and Mary coach us to success. We can't wait to launch this book as part of our school curriculum and in our salons. BGTD!!!!!*

– Wanda Williams-Woods, The Salon Professional Academy, Nashville, TN

―――――――――

Wow! So powerful! It was amazing! We have grown so much from this! This has been a tool to keep us growing, staying on top! Written in a language that stylists and students can relate to, Over The Top *has given us a new way to look at how we create exceptional guest experiences. We had a lot of fun going through the lessons. The 'ahas' and discoveries were put immediately into action with immediate results!* Over The Top *has helped our students build confidence in offering add-on services, chemicals, retail, and rebooks. We have seen our students reach their goals faster. Our guests have commented on how they have seen a difference in their consultations and follow-ups. Our students now understand the difference between creating looks and just doing hair! Michael and Mary—this is just what our industry needed—we are so grateful and touched by you!*

– Brady Snider, PCI Academy, Ames, IA

To have a passion in life is one of the strongest emotions we can have, to experience it every day is a gift, and to earn our living doing it is the blessing only a few of us discover…hairdressing for me is all of the above. I am in awe of the stylists who will read this book, learn from this book, and have an amazing career and life because of this book…With respect and gratitude to Michael and Mary Cole.

– Kris Sorbie, President, kris sorbie LLC and Redken 5th Avenue NYC Education Artistic Director

―――――――――

We have worked with Michael Cole for many years. Lately we have been beta testing Over The Top *in both our schools. Once again Michael touches on the truths and the heart of our beautiful industry.* Over The Top *meets the needs of today's students, educators, and owners. We recommend all SSBC materials, but especially Michael's latest creation,* Over The Top, *for its real world yet fun approach to the business of beauty. We have to do whatever it takes to prepare the next generation of our industry, and Michael and Mary Cole continue to have that purpose as well. God bless them!*

– Mary Clare Lokken, PCI Academy, Ames, IA

―――――――――

As a Summit Salon Academy, we pride ourselves on a higher level of education. Over The Top *provides our students with the perfect resource and teaching tool to transform their passion of artistry into a successful salon career.*

– Joanne Powers, Owner, Summit Salon Academy, Tampa, FL

There is no one else in our great industry who has worked harder to provide the beauty professional with themes, ideas, and fundamentals that will not only make them better, but make them rich at the same time. This book can take you over the top. I will not only use it as a textbook, I will give it to those close to me and suggest it to all of my colleagues. This book will be on all of my booklists.

– Geno Stampora, Stampora Consulting, Inc.

Over The Top *is full of simple but profound principles that you can immediately put into practice to achieve the income of a Top 20 stylist. Michael and Mary's thirty years of salon experience and genuine care for stylists shows up on every page. It is a brilliantly written book that will inspire you daily. The financial difference it'll make for you will be amazing and the service experience it'll make for your guests will be extraordinary.* Over The Top *has become an essential part of Redken's educational foundation and a cornerstone of Redken's business programs.*

– Bobbi Foster-Kelly, Retired AVP, National Training, Redken/Pureology

Michael and Mary Cole have done it again with this visually exciting learning experience, Over The Top*! I believe this book is the most powerful tool that has ever been developed to connect the dots between being creative behind the chair, applying success principles, and understanding how to stay on the fast and furious path to success. The interactive exercises are brilliant, challenging, applicable, and fun!*

– Kristi Valenzuela, Director, Products & Sales, Summit Salon Business Center

In Over The Top *stylists, students, and educators will find what it takes to win. If you want to be a Top 20, enjoy this masterpiece and WIN, WIN, WIN!*

– Angela Lema, Co-owner, Salon Professional Academy, Grand Junction, CO

Over The Top *is not just a home run, it's a grand slam! It will assist a hairdresser/service provider to a very successful career, but more impressively, it will assist them to be a true market leader!*

– Frank Gambuzza, President of Intercoiffure America/Canada, Owner, Salon Visage, Knoxville, Tennessee

Over The Top *is like no other resource available to stylists and students. It not only gives tools needed to reveal your full potential, it is filled with exercises and worksheets that will help you get there fast. You will love the versatility of* Over The Top *and how it speaks to you, the learner. The easy-to-follow lesson plans allow* Over The Top *to be utilized individually or in a group setting. You will refer to it time and time again. This is a must-have for all stylists and students who desire success. Thank you, Michael and Mary, for your time and dedication and for being difference makers.*

– Sonja Plunkett, Vice President at The Salon Professional Academy Franchise

After 10,000 coaching sessions with stylists all over the country, I'm super-excited to utilize the Over The Top *stylist training guide! It's packed with innovative content, visual realism, and awesome discussion topics for each chapter. It's the ultimate coaching and mentoring guide for owners, managers, and coaches!*

– Gavin Salsbery, Stockholder, Board Member, and Consultant, Summit Salon Business Center

Over The Top *will escalate your career to new heights. Whether you are in cosmetology school, an independent contractor, or a member of a salon team, following the steps outlined here will make you laugh, make you think, and make it impossible for you not to succeed.*

– Randy & Sharon Kunkel, Co-Founders Summit Salon Business Center and KRS Sales Development

INTRODUCTION

When we graduated from barber and beauty school in 1974, we never imagined that we would have the tremendous opportunity to bring this kind of profound knowledge to salon stylists. This textbook took us almost five years to complete, not because we couldn't get it finished, but because we wanted it to contain everything stylists would need to know in order to have the kind of career they've always dreamed of.

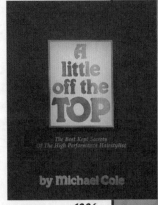

1986

Our first book, *A Little Off The Top*, published in 1986, taught thousands of salon stylists how to make more money. It became the foundation for a course called "Boot Camp." Nearly twenty years later, in 2004, we published *A Little More Off The Top*, and it was received with unprecedented success.

One of our intentions has always been to make sure that we're both living what we teach and so the idea of always striving to better our best is a principle we practice. There were many times while creating this book that trying to better our best darn near drove us crazy. But Our Calling to serve salon stylists in this way inspired us to once again write a new book, *Over The Top*.

2004

What makes *Over The Top* extraordinary is that we took the best of our previous two books and combined it with an enormous amount of new learning we gained from training stylists. We then designed it with hundreds of humorous color illustrations, and packed it full of scripts, examples, charts, and exercises to create the easy, fast, and fun book you have in your hands right now!

If you are a student reading, studying, and practicing the principles of this book, your ride in school will not only be more relevant, practical, and fun, but you will be able to hit the ground running the moment you start working in the salon and you will experience growth and success faster than you ever dreamed possible.

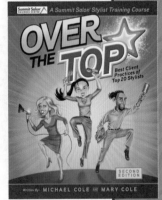

2011

If you're already a salon stylist, it's important to both of us that as you read, study, and practice the principles of *Over The Top,* you experience a renewed energy in your career and enjoy financial jumps in your take-home pay.

Whether you're in school or already behind the chair, make the decision to take daily action on the ideas in this book and watch your income explode!

Michael and Mary Cole

One of the major turning points in the CAREER of any Stylist is the day they no longer feel rejected or embarrassed when guests say 'no' to any of the three recommendations they're making (retail, additional services, or rebook).

Many Stylists will go through their entire career without reaching that turning point, and as a result they stop talking about retail, add-on services, and rebooking.

For Stylists who have this realization, OMG is their freaking dynamite booming and their CAREER will go OVER THE TOP!

–Michael Cole

Golden Rule of 80/20

How fast and far we grow our income will always be determined by the path we're on—Bottom 80 or Top 20. As we develop our understanding of the 80/20 Rule, the power in us to earn $1,000,000 more over the life of our career is unleashed. This is why learning about the Golden Rule of 80/20 and the attitudes and actions of a Top 20 Stylist is vital to our success.

KEY POINTS

- The 80/20 Rule
- Penalties & Payoffs
- Top 20 Potential
- Career or Job
- Top 20 Smart Parts
- Money Smart, Guest Smart, Self Smart
- B.Y.O.W.—Bring Your Own Willingness
- Stubbornness: The Thief of Prosperity

TOP 20

1 WHY IS IT THAT...

... two cosmetology graduates coming out of the same school at the same time ...

... who go to work in the same salon, earning the same commission ...

... receiving the same number of new guests, and yet ...

... at the end of five years one stylist has earned $100,000 MORE than the other?

ANSWER: THE 80/20 RULE!

1. THE GOLDEN RULE OF 80/20

The Golden Rule of 80/20 says that **20%** of the stylists working in salons are retaining **80%** of the request guests, selling **80%** of the services and products, and as result are taking home **80%** of the money. **These are Top 20 stylists.**

The rule's **opposite** is also true. You'll find that **80%** of stylists who work in that same salon are only retaining **20%** of the request guests, selling only **20%** of the services and products and consequently are only taking home **20%** of the money. **These are Bottom 80 stylists.**

The career of a Top 20 stylist is golden because it's **80%** richer in money, happiness, and success than the career of a Bottom 80. Top 20s grow **80%** faster than stylists who are stuck in Bottom 80.

The purpose of *Over The Top: Best Guest Practices of Top 20 Stylists* is to help stylists achieve greater financial success by learning the ways of Top 20s and avoiding the pitfalls of Bottom 80.

Top 20s
thrive!
and
Bottom 80s
SURVIVE.

3

2. PENALTIES AND PAYOFFS

This chart illustrates the penalties for being stuck in Bottom 80 and the payoffs for becoming Top 20. Look at the dramatic jumps in income with Top 20s and notice the $35,000 wall that Bottom 80s hit after the third year. This is when Top 20s really start out-earning Bottom 80s. As a result Top 20s will earn almost **$100,000 more in the first five years** and **$1,000,000 more over a 25-year career!** This is why it's so important to learn the ways of Top 20!

BOTTOM 80	ANNUAL STYLIST INCOME/YEAR	TOP 20
Under $20,000	1st Year	Over $25,000
Under $25,000	2nd Year	Over $35,000
Under $30,000	3rd Year	Over $45,000
Under $35,000	4th Year	Over $55,000
Under $35,000	5th Year	Over $75,000
Under $145,000	5 Year Total	Over $235,000

3. TOP 20 POTENTIAL

If we look around, we will see plenty of people who are Top 20 in plenty of ways. In schools we see Top 20 Teachers as well as Top 20 Students. In salons we see Top 20 Leaders and Top 20 Stylists. In all areas of life there are opportunities to be Top 20s. There are Top 20 Cooks, Athletes, Doctors, Parents, there are <u>Top 20s for everything!</u>

Here's the good news: we all have the potential to be Top 20 Stylists! **As a matter of fact, "so-called" Bottom 80 stylists are really unconscious and underdeveloped Top 20s.** While all of us have the potential of becoming a Top 20, not all of us believe we can, or know how to do it. As we go through the book we will learn to recognize Bottom 80 behaviors and what it takes to become a Top 20 Stylist.

No one ever needs to be pushed aside!

There is plenty of room for ***ALL OF US TO BE TOP 20!***

TIME FOR ACTION!

1. How would your life be different than it is right now if you could earn $10,000 more a year?

2. Name someone you know who is a Top 20.

3. Describe what makes that person a Top 20.

4. Why is having Top 20s in your life important?

4. **THE 80/20 IN ALL OF US**

There's no such thing as a "Bottom 80" or "Top 20" stylist because there's a Top 20 and a Bottom 80 in all of us. Sometimes we're in Top 20 **BLUE** and sometimes we fall into Bottom 80 **RED**. In other words, there's a **Bottom 80 Self** and a **Top 20 Self** in all of us and it shows up in two entirely different kinds of thoughts, attitudes, and actions. Some of us show more of our Top 20 Self and less Bottom 80 and some of us show more of our Bottom 80 Self and less Top 20.

Being stuck in Bottom 80 **RED** doesn't make us bad people or bad stylists. It just prevents us from having a great career.

If we want all of the success that comes with a great career, we must develop the awareness and skills to keep us in Top 20 **BLUE** longer and get out of Bottom 80 **RED** quicker.

TIME FOR ACTION!

1. **Describe your attitude and actions when you are stuck in Bottom 80 RED.**

2. **How are your attitudes and actions different when you are in Top 20 BLUE?**

5. CAREER OR JOB

Most of us begin our career in Top 20 **BLUE**, motivated to learn, grow, and succeed. But somewhere along the way, many of us fall into Bottom 80 **RED** and our career crumbles into a job. Let's look at how this happens when we use the **Frame** to show the connection between what we SEE, what we FEEL, what we DO, and what we GET.

CAREER

In Top 20 **BLUE** we SEE our work life as a career.

Career: A profession we <u>CHOOSE</u>, <u>TRAIN FOR</u>, and <u>PURSUE</u> as a life work with the intention to succeed.

We FEEL hopeful, excited, and inspired about our chosen career. We DO our best to create an extraordinary experience for our guests. As a result, we GET more money, have more fun, and have the satisfaction of knowing that we have achieved a great CAREER.

TOP 20 "CAREER"

CAREER	Hopeful, Excited, Inspired
Prosperity, Abundance, Joy	Create an extraordinary experience for our guests

JOB

When we're stuck in Bottom 80 RED we SEE our work life as a job.

Job: Any work we <u>HAVE</u> to do in order to make enough money to live.

We FEEL bored, annoyed, and trapped in our job. We DO ordinary work, getting guests in and out. As a result, we GET a dead-end, boring job with enough money to survive. That's why the word JOB stands for... ***Just Over Broke!***

BOTTOM 80 "JOB"

JOB	Bored, Annoyed, Trapped
Stuck, Broke	Just enough to get by

How we SEE our livelihood is the biggest difference between stylists in Top 20 Careers and stylists stuck in Bottom 80 Jobs. Stylists in Top 20 **BLUE** have developed a better attitude about what they do for a living, and it's that kind of thinking that leads them to a prosperous career and an extraordinary life.

When you change your thinking, you change your life!

TIME FOR ACTION!

1. **Describe what a Top 20 career looks like to you.**

6. TOP 20 SMART PARTS

Top 20s know that to make a lot of money and have a great career they must become smarter. The Top 20 Smart Parts include:

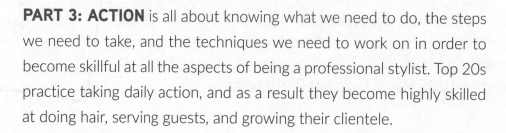

PART 1: AWARENESS means being wide-awake. Top 20s have a keen sense of self-awareness, which is the ability to see their strengths and weaknesses and what they need to work at to get better.

PART 2: ATTITUDE is made of our mental emotional energy. One of the most important things that Top 20s are keenly aware of is the quality of their own attitude, their mental and emotional energy, and the enormous influence their attitude has on their overall success.

PART 3: ACTION is all about knowing what we need to do, the steps we need to take, and the techniques we need to work on in order to become skillful at all the aspects of being a professional stylist. Top 20s practice taking daily action, and as a result they become highly skilled at doing hair, serving guests, and growing their clientele.

These three Smart Parts energize our career by showing us the connection between **learning more and earning more**. The moment we make the commitment to develop the awareness, attitude, and actions for greater success, a tremendous power is unleashed in us to experience sudden and dramatic jumps in our personal income.

7. MONEY, GUEST, AND SELF SMART

Top 20 Stylists are able to achieve much higher levels of personal income because they are always applying the **Smart Parts** to managing three of the most important relationships in their life: their relationship with **money**, their relationship with **guests**, and the relationship they have with **themselves**.

MONEY SMART is the ability to achieve dramatic and sudden jumps in personal income by improving our relationship with money and how we handle it. Top 20s are Money Smart. They are highly skillful at managing their appointment book in ways that allow them **to make the most amount of money in the quickest period of time with the least amount of stress.**

GUEST SMART is the ability to build great relationships with guests by knowing how to communicate effectively. Top 20s are Guest Smart with all of their guests. They are extremely skillful at selling services and retail, rebooking, and getting referrals. **As a result, Top 20s build a great repeat clientele and earn a much higher income.**

SELF SMART is about having a great relationship with ourselves. It's having the personal awareness and skill to maintain a great attitude and radiate positive energy. Top 20s are Self Smart. They are truly skillful at maintaining positive attitudes and overcoming negative attitudes that cause failure. **Top 20s are self-confident, self-motivated, and self-disciplined.** They accept responsibility without blame, are able to stay cool under pressure, and bounce back after disappointments.

Stylists who are stuck in Bottom 80 are unaware and unskilled in these three essential areas, and as a result make less money, lose more guests, and experience chaos, drama, and scarcity in their personal lives. **Getting out of Bottom 80 RED quicker and staying in Top 20 BLUE longer requires us to become Money Smart, Guest Smart, and Self Smart.**

MONEY SMART	GUEST SMART	SELF SMART

Develop the AWARENESS, ATTITUDE, and ACTIONS to...

MONEY SMART	GUEST SMART	SELF SMART
• Make the most amount of money in the quickest period of time with the least amount of stress. • Achieve dramatic and sudden jumps in personal income. • Control and balance personal spending with earning.	• Communicate with guests effectively. • Sell services and retail. • Rebook guests. • Get referrals. • Build clientele. • Balance personal and professional conversations.	• Maintain and radiate a positive attitude. • Overcome negative attitudes. • Be self-confident, self-motivated, and self-disciplined. • Accept responsibility without blame. • Stay cool under pressure. Bounce back after disappointments.

TIME FOR ACTION!

	From the chart above, choose one SMART action for MONEY, GUEST, and SELF that you want to improve.	How would that make a difference in your life?
MONEY SMART		
GUEST SMART		
SELF SMART		

8. B.Y.O.W.—BRING YOUR OWN WILLINGNESS

If we willingly engage in learning the **Best Guest Practices** contained in this book, we will be absolutely delighted before we are halfway through. We will be on the road to becoming Top 20s and enjoying a career that promises greater financial success. But in order for this to happen we must bring an Attitude of Willingness to every lesson in the *Over The Top* program. **Willingness is a personal thing, and no one can make us willing; it is something we must decide for ourselves.**

Willingness means having an open mind to the ideas presented in this book accompanied by an enthusiastic desire to take action. We must also have the Willingness to disobey the FEAR that comes with taking action on these new ideas. We call this kind of Willingness COURAGE—**the courage to go outside of our comfort zone.**

COURAGE:
The willingness to disobey the fear that comes with taking new actions.

9. STUBBORNNESS: THE THIEF OF PROSPERITY

The opposite of Willingness is Stubbornness. Stubbornness is the Thief of Prosperity because it robs us of opportunities for greater income, keeping us stuck in Bottom 80. Many of us are totally unaware of our stubbornness. Anytime anyone offers us a suggestion to improve our self or our business behind the chair, we stubbornly reject it by saying, "Leave us alone we're F. I. N. E." We're fine alright, we're **F**reaked out, **I**n debt, **N**ot making enough, and **E**motionally stressed.

Many veteran stylists stubbornly believe that it's too late for them and they'll never get ahead. But here's the truth: **It's *never* too late. We can make up for lost time!** We can step up and jump ahead. As veteran stylists, we have the potential to earn over $100,000 more in the next five years, over $200,000 in the next ten. We even have the potential to earn $500,000 more in the next twenty years.

TIME FOR ACTION!

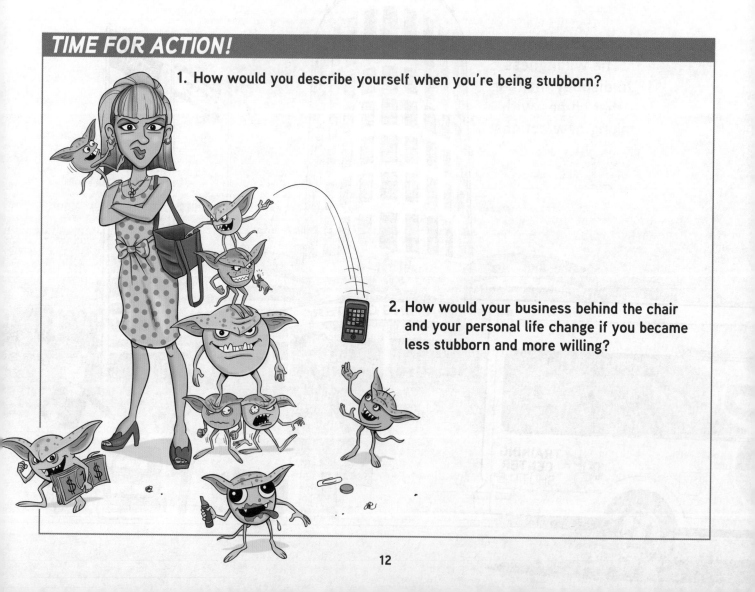

1. How would you describe yourself when you're being stubborn?

2. How would your business behind the chair and your personal life change if you became less stubborn and more willing?

GOLDEN RULE OF 80/20 SUMMARY

How fast and far we grow our income will always be determined by what path we're on... Bottom 80 **RED** or Top 20 **BLUE**. There is growth on the Bottom 80 path. The problem is that it occurs slowly and in small amounts over long periods of time. On the other hand, growth on the Top 20 path happens more quickly, in larger amounts, over shorter periods of time. Becoming a Top 20 Stylist begins with developing a new set of attitudes starting with the Attitude of Willingness. Becoming a Top 20 requires us to demonstrate an Attitude of Willingness by keeping the following three promises.

PROMISE #1	PROMISE #2	PROMISE #3
To believe in ourselves, in our potential to be Top 20, and in our own worthiness to have a great career.	*To keep an open mind by being receptive to new ideas.*	*To immediately put into practice the ideas that we learn.*

Keeping these promises puts us and keeps us on the Fast Track To Wealth, where we earn $1,000,000 more over the life of an extraordinary career. So if we're willing to believe in our potential to be a Top 20 Stylist, then we're ready to step up into greater levels of success.

The moment we demonstrate the COURAGE to become LESS STUBBORN and MORE WILLING, we UNLEASH THE POWER of our TOP 20 POTENTIAL to explode!

TOP 20 LIFE DREAM SHEET

Create a
Top 20 profile
of yourself.

What does your
Top 20 lifestyle
look like?

What does your
Top 20 career
look like?

What do your
Top 20 relationships
look like?

1. On the LEFT SIDE, color in the numbered light bulb that indicates your current level of stubbornness.

2. On the RIGHT SIDE, color in the numbered light bulb you would be willing to reduce your stubbornness to.

The *Stubbornness Tester* rates our current level of stubbornness.

10 represents TOTALLY stubborn and 1 is KINDA-SORTA stubbornness.

3. What are some salon situations where your stubbornness comes up and gets in the way of you earning more money?

4. How could you practice being less stubborn and more willing in this area?

5. What kind of difference would that make in your life?

TAKING MY CAREER *OVER THE TOP* DECLARATION

I _____ PROMISE...
    NAME

to demonstrate my willingness to reveal and develop MORE of my Top 20 Self by:

⭐ believing in my potential and my worthiness to have a great career.

⭐ keeping an open mind and staying receptive to the ideas in this book.

⭐ being an active participant in the class during discussions and activities.

⭐ completing all assignments and exercises.

⭐ being prepared for class.

⭐ putting into action what I learned.

⭐ having the courage to disobey my fears.

⭐ supporting and encouraging my co-workers.

SIGNATURE: _____   DATE: _____

BIG 4

Becoming more skillful at any one of the Big 4, (Service, Retail, Repeat, or Referral) automatically empowers us to make more money, but it's having the right combination of the Big 4 that unlocks the power to achieve the sudden and dramatic jumps in our personal income that we all desire.

Top 20 Stylists often earn *3–5 times more money* than Bottom 80s because they are highly skilled in all aspects of the Big 4. This is why learning about the Big 4 is essential to our greater financial success.

KEY POINTS

- Big 4
- Service
- Retail
- Repeat
- Referral
- Dialing in the Right Combination

2 HAVE YOU EVER HAD...

...one of those awesome weeks when everything went incredibly well?
All of your favorite guests came in, and they bought extra services and retail like crazy.

You even got a handful
of referrals who couldn't
wait to see you.

And at the end of the week
you were blown away by how
much money you made.

**What you experienced was the
powerful combination of
the *Big 4* coming together
to create a perfect week.**

1. THE BIG 4

The Big 4 are the four individual ways that we make money behind the chair: **Service**, **Retail**, **Repeat**, and **Referral**. When unlocked and mixed together, the Big 4 become an explosive combination! Any time our guests make the decision to buy more services and more products, come back to see us, and send in a referral, we make more money. Each one contributes in its own unique way to our greater financial growth and requires its own set of skills. Therefore, we need to take a closer look at each of these four revenue streams.

2. SERVICE

The majority of our income comes from the services we perform on our guests. The ability to sell and perform more **services** is the number one key to developing the right combination of the Big 4, because guests who get more **services** also buy more **retail**, rebook more often as **repeat guests**, and send us more **referrals**.

Services include haircut, color, texturizing, relaxing, conditioning, styling, and waxing. When we become highly skilled in selling and performing more services to our guests, it substantially raises our income by increasing our **dollars per ticket**. Chemical services earn us more money per minute than just cutting hair, allowing us to earn more money while serving fewer guests. Having the sales ability to influence guests to buy chemical services and additional services like waxing, treatments, extra foils, and glazes is a smart way to increase our income.

80/20 SERVICE COMPARISONS

BOTTOM 80	TOP 20
▶ Believe that if a guest wants a service they will ask for it, and if they don't, they won't.	▶ Believe that the ability to offer great services to their guests is the foundation of a successful career.
▶ Unwilling to attend training and get little out of those they are forced to attend. As a result they have average service skills.	▶ Willingly attend training and come away highly skilled in all aspects of chemical and additional services.
▶ Afraid that they'll talk a guest into doing something they aren't good at.	▶ Know that even if they are unsure they are willing to ask for help.
▶ Only able to offer a limited range of looks and services. Condemned to earn average income from their inability to offer services.	▶ Have the ability to offer a wider range of new looks and services. Earn a greater income because they do 3–5 times more services on fewer guests.

TIME FOR ACTION!

1. Look at the **BOTTOM 80 SERVICE COMPARISON** list and pick the one you can relate to the most.

2. List a service skill that you need to improve upon in order to make more money.

3. How would improving that service skill enable you to offer a wider range of looks and services to your guests?

4. How would improving that particular service skill influence your guests to:

   a. *Buy more retail?*

   b. *Rebook their next appointment?*

   c. *Send in referrals?*

3. RETAIL

The second way we earn money is from the retail products our guests purchase from us. Retail products can be put into three categories:

1 HOME HAIRCARE
All shampoos and conditioners

2 STYLING AIDS
Styling products such as sprays, gels, and mousses

3 STYLING TOOLS
brushes, irons, dryers, etc.

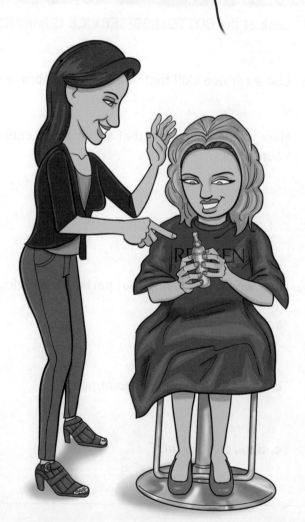

Becoming highly skilled at using, teaching, and selling retail products to our guests is essential to developing the right combination of the Big 4. Teaching guests **what to do** and **what to use** to recreate their look at home influences them to **buy retail products** from us. More importantly, teaching our guests to style their hair gives them an extraordinary experience, gets them to rebook future services with us as repeat guests, and inspires them to send us referrals. So we see once again how success with one of the Big 4 is linked to our success with the other three.

80/20 RETAIL COMPARISONS

Bottom 80	Top 20
▶ Believe that retail products are pretty much all the same, and take the products they use for granted.	▶ Believe that the retail products they use are essential tools for creating the looks their guests want.
▶ See product knowledge training as pointless, boring, and a waste of time.	▶ Make product knowledge training a high priority and, as a result, are well trained in all aspects of retail.
▶ Are unskilled, unable, and uninterested in teaching guests to understand and use their retail products.	▶ Are highly skilled in teaching guests to use great retail products and tools to recreate their look.
▶ View retail as "pushy" selling and instead spend all their time making friends with guests.	▶ Know that teaching their guests to use retail products is essential to building a Top 20 clientele.
▶ Sell little retail, retain fewer guests, and earn a lot less money.	▶ Sell 3-5 times more retail, retain more guests, and earn substantially more money.

TIME FOR ACTION!

1. Look at the **Bottom 80** retail comparisons list and pick the one you can relate to most.

2. How is that particular belief or attitude holding you back from selling retail?

3. How would improving your knowledge of retail products influence your ability to teach guests to recreate their look?

4. How does offering your guests retail affect your success at service, repeat, and referral?

4. **REPEAT**

The third way we earn money is from the new guests who rebook with us as our repeat guests. Having a solid base of repeat guests is essential to developing the right combination of the Big 4. **As our base of repeat guests grows, we have more guests to sell our services and retail to, as well as more guests to get referrals from.**

Top 20s are highly skilled at turning new guests into repeat guests and as a result quickly build a great clientele and are less dependent on walk-ins. Stylists stuck in Bottom 80 are untrained, unaware, and unskilled at building repeat business. They are dependent on a Busy Bus of walk-ins to show up, believing it is the salon's responsibility to continue feeding them new guests.

80/20 REPEAT COMPARISONS

Bottom 80	Top 20
▶ See clientele development training as pointless, boring, and a waste of time.	▶ Are well trained in all aspects of building a repeat clientele.
▶ Take new guests for granted, depend on walk-ins, and never seem to get enough.	▶ Don't take new guests for granted and see them as opportunities to build a repeat guest.
▶ Are unskilled, unable, and uninterested in turning new guests into repeat guests.	▶ Are highly skilled in turning new guests into repeat guests.
▶ Give new guests an ordinary service experience.	▶ Create an extraordinary experience for every guest they serve.
▶ Retain only 20% of the new guests they receive and never build a full repeat clientele.	▶ Retain 80% or more of the new guests they receive and build a full clientele in two years.

TIME FOR ACTION!

1. What makes an experience EXTRAORDINARY for a guest?

2. What makes an experience ORDINARY for a guest?

3. Why is being dependent on salon walk-ins a bad habit to have?

4. What's the connection between being skillful at service and retail and the ability to turn new guests into repeat guests?

5. REFERRALS

The fourth way we make money is from guests who have been referred to us by our repeat guests. When we become highly skilled at getting referrals, we increase our income by continuing to grow our repeat guest base. We naturally lose guests over time and referrals are much more likely to return to us as repeat guests, which once again make us less dependent on walk-ins. Having a steady stream of referral guests is crucial to developing the right combination of the Big 4. **Referrals purchase more services and retail, rebook as repeat guests, and send in even more referrals.**

5 One initial referral offering can lead to more referrals, more services, more retail, more repeat guests, and more MONEY!

4 ...and send in four more referrals!

3 Two friends get great new looks...

1 Stylist asks for referrals

2 Guest sends in two referrals.

80/20 REFERRAL COMPARISONS

▶ Believe it's not their responsibility to get referrals and so they remain dependent on walk-ins.	▶ Believe that their ability to get referrals is essential to building repeat clientele.
▶ Are untrained, unskilled, and uninterested, and see asking for referrals as "begging."	▶ Are well trained in all aspects of referral building.
▶ Are afraid to promote themselves to get referrals.	▶ Promote themselves to get referrals.
▶ Stay stale, stuck, and in the rut of guest complacency.	▶ Grow faster because they attract guests who want all the services offered and are willing to pay for them.

TIME FOR ACTION!

1. What are some of the ways we can lose a repeat guest?

2. Look at the Bottom 80 referral comparisons list and pick the one you can relate to most.

3. How is that particular belief or attitude holding you back from greater success?

4. What can you do to promote yourself?

BIG 4 SUMMARY

The Big 4 are the four individual ways that we make money behind the chair, **Service**, **Retail**, **Repeat**, and **Referral**. Any time our guests make the decision to buy more services and more products, come back to see us, and send in referrals, we make more money. We all have the potential of earning as much as a million dollars more over the lifetime of our career by becoming highly skilled at the Big 4.

Getting better at any one of the Big 4 automatically empowers us to make more money, but it's our skillfulness at creating the **right combination** of the Big 4 that guarantees us sudden and dramatic jumps from Bottom 80 to Top 20 in our personal income.

TOP 20 SERVICE MENU SHEET

Use this page to come up with as many services for each of the categories as you can think of. Write down how much you would charge for each service.

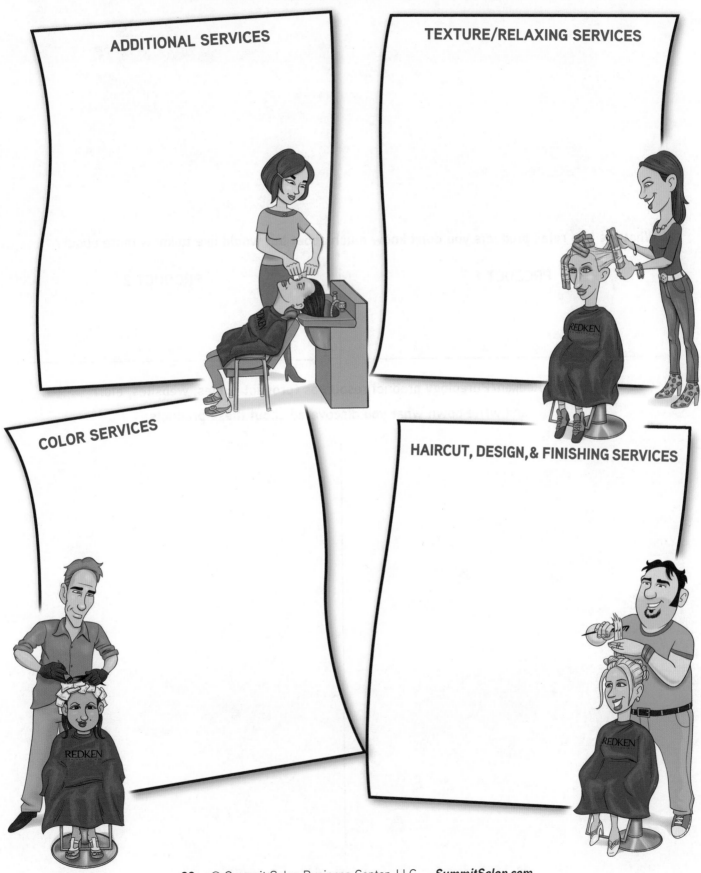

ADDITIONAL SERVICES

TEXTURE/RELAXING SERVICES

COLOR SERVICES

HAIRCUT, DESIGN,& FINISHING SERVICES

PRODUCT SMART

1. What are your favorite retail products and why?

2. What are two retail products you don't know much about but would like to know more about?

<table>
<tr><td>PRODUCT 1</td><td>PRODUCT 2</td></tr>
<tr><td>_____</td><td>_____</td></tr>
</table>

Use the Redken/Pureology product resources (product guides, websites, etc.)
and write down what you discovered about these products.

BUILDING A REPEAT CLIENTELE

What do you like about repeat guests?

TREASURING REFERRAL GUESTS

How do you feel when you get a referral?

What makes referrals special?

Power Wheel

Enjoying tremendous jumps in our financial income demands that we give as much attention to developing our Guest Communication Skills as we do to our Technical Skills.

Top 20s know that the overwhelming majority of their financial success not only lies in their ability to design, color, and finish hair, but more importantly in their ability to communicate in a way that influences their guests to buy more services and retail, rebook their next appointment, and send in referrals.

Because they understand the importance of being highly skilled at guest communication, Top 20s have made the Power Wheel a big part of their chair side manner, and as a result earn 3–5 times more money than stylists stuck in Bottom 80.

KEY POINTS

- Power Wheel
- Inside of Power Wheel
- Outside of Power Wheel
- The Bicycle
- Wheels Working Together
- The Formula for Success
- Building a Stronger Back Wheel
- Building a Stronger Front Wheel

3 WHAT'S THE SECRET TO...

... doing great hair, having a full book, AND MAKING LOTS OF MONEY?

Having the willingness to build your TOP 20 **TECHNICAL SKILLS** *and* **GUEST COMMUNICATION SKILLS!**

Developing these two sets together gives you tremendous POWER to succeed.

1. THE POWER WHEEL

The Power Wheel is an amazing guest handling system that takes the stress and strain out of communicating effectively with guests. It covers the entire guest visit from beginning to end, guaranteeing that the experience guests have is an **extraordinary one**.

As we become skillful at working the Power Wheel, we go from being forgetful and scattered to focusing on and talking about what's important. The Power Wheel makes selling services and retail more natural and less intimidating. It takes away feelings of fear, stress, and worry and empowers us with courage and self-confidence.

2. TWO SIDES OF THE POWER WHEEL

There are two sides that make up the Power Wheel, inside and outside.

THE INSIDE OF THE POWER WHEEL

At the center of the Power Wheel is the Top 20 Star which represents the unlimited positive energy we all possess called **Star Power**. It's made up of the **positive thoughts, beliefs, attitudes, and feelings** we have about ourselves and our guests.

There is a direct connection between explosions in our personal income and developing our Top 20 Star Power. **The positive energy of our Star Power has an enormous influence on the experience our guests have when they're sitting in our chair.** Guests love buying services and products from stylists who have great attitudes. The better our attitude is, the greater experience our guests have and the more money they are willing to spend. Nothing turns off that willingness to spend faster than a Bottom 80 attitude. **In other words, our attitude is either making us or costing us a lot of money.** For that reason we must make developing our Star Power as important as learning to do great hair.

THE OUTSIDE OF THE POWER WHEEL

The outside of the Power Wheel is made up of five parts: **Bonding, Consulting, Servicing, Finishing, and Evolving.** These five parts make up the guest handling system. **It's what we say or do to positively communicate with our guests.** While each of the five parts contains its own set of skills, each part is connected to the other parts, which makes the system complete.

3. BONDING

Bonding is all about building credibility and rapport quickly. Bonding is our first real opportunity to start building credibility by making positive and lasting first impressions. It's our chance to connect with our guests so that they immediately feel comfortable and confident with us. These kinds of positive impressions give our guests great feelings about the money they're going to be spending on our services and products. Top 20s never underestimate the power of becoming better at Bonding with guests.

4. CONSULTING

Consulting is where we help our guests find a look they want, and offer the services they need to create that look. The main reason our guests don't buy more services and product, rebook, or send in referrals is because they feel we didn't listen to them or we didn't understand or appreciate the look they wanted. Nothing closes the gap of misunderstanding what our guest wants better than a Top 20 Consultation.

5. SERVICING

The Servicing process is the longest part of a guest's appointment and it provides us with a number of opportunities to use our technical and communication skills in ways that make our guests look and feel great. We do this by keeping the guest involved with a balance of social and professional conversations. Servicing is also where we introduce home haircare and rebooking. Developing Top 20 Servicing skills guarantees our guest an extraordinary experience with us, but is also a major key to achieving sudden and dramatic jumps in personal income.

6. FINISHING

In Finishing we teach our guests what we do and use to make their look work for them. When our guest's look starts coming together, they feel the extraordinary energy of the service experience and their excitement builds. It's that energy and good feeling that leads to higher retail sales, more rebooks, repeats, and referrals. Top 20s are keenly aware of the power their Finishing skills have on their guests and their ability to build a successful clientele.

7. EVOLVING

Evolving is the fifth step of the Power Wheel and it is best defined as achieving big jumps in take home pay by building a repeat clientele through the activity of Guest Planning. There are two ways to grow a repeat clientele, Naturally and Supernaturally. Natural Growth occurs slowly and in small amounts over long periods of time. Supernatural Growth occurs quickly and in large amounts over shorter periods of time.

It's about growing our business in spite of the economic conditions by creating our own busy season. Top 20s enjoy Supernatural Growth because they engage an essential activity called Guest Planning.

8. FULL CIRCLE SUCCESS

The Power Wheel is our system for building an awesome repeat clientele and a great income. Nothing significant happens in our lives without radical change, and this is no exception. The change in this case will be in our attitude and our effort at learning to use the Power Wheel. If our effort is half-hearted, it will be worse than no effort at all. **When we make the commitment to become skillful at using the Power Wheel and combine it with our Technical Skills, we will experience a level of financial success that few stylists will ever have the opportunity to know.**

TIME FOR ACTION!

1. What are some of the challenges you face when communicating with guests?

2. How would learning about the Power Wheel help you with those challenges?

3. Which part of the Power Wheel are you most curious about?

9. THE BICYCLE

The two wheels on a bicycle are a great way of representing our Technical Skills and our Client Communication Skills. How well these two wheels work together will determine how quickly we move to Top 20.

The back wheel represents our Technical Skills. This includes the techniques we use to create great looks on our guests: from cutting and design to coloring, texturizing, relaxing, and conditioning as well as product knowledge.

The front wheel represents our Guest Communication Skills within the Power Wheel. This includes the conversations and consultations we have with our guests and the service and retail offerings we make.

39

10. BACK WHEEL

The back wheel represents our Technical Skills because the purpose of the back wheel is to give the bicycle the power to move in a forward direction. Having strong Technical Skills gives us that same power to keep our personal income moving forward because we:

- *Have a much greater range of looks to offer our guests.*

- *Become highly skilled at creating great looks that guests love.*

- *Are able to explain to our guests what we are doing in ways that get and keep them interested.*

- *Stay on the leading edge with up-to-date fashion, new products, and advanced techniques.*

11. FRONT WHEEL

The front wheel represents the Guest Communication Skills of the Power Wheel. The purpose of the front wheel is completely different. We use the front wheel of the bicycle to steer and guide our guests in the direction we want them to go. The front wheel is all about our ability to gain greater control over the conversations we have with our guests by:

- *Learning to balance social conversations with conversations around the Big 4 (service, retail, repeat, referral).*

- *Having a well-developed Top 20 vocabulary.*

- *Developing the ability to sell services and products.*

- *Being able to influence new guests to rebook as repeats.*

- *Persuading guests to send in referrals.*

- *Understanding the look the guest wants.*

- *Confidently handling difficult, confused, and unsure guests.*

12. **WHEELS WORKING TOGETHER**

For a bicycle to operate at peak performance, both wheels must be top-of-the-line with advanced technology and in excellent condition. That same idea holds true for us as well. For us to reach Top 20 financial performance in the quickest amount of time, our Technical and our Guest Communication Skills must be top- of-the-line with advanced training and working together in excellent condition.

13. **SEEING THE CONNECTION**

There is a much bigger connection between back wheel Technical Skills and front wheel Guest Communication Skills than many of us realize.

As we develop our Technical Skills, we automatically expand the range of **looks, services, and products** we can offer to the guests who sit in our chair. Whenever we attend any kind of technical training programs, we learn great methods and techniques for cutting, coloring, conditioning, and finishing hair. **But that's not all there is to learn.**

We also have the opportunity to learn the very **language** the trainer uses to explain and describe what they are teaching. Top 20 Stylists use that same language when they are communicating with their guests to confidently explain and describe what's possible for their guest's hair.

TOP 20 GOALS FOR ATTENDING TECHNICAL CLASSES

Learn as much as possible about the technique.

Listen for the words and language and write down some of the ways trainers describe and explain what they're doing.

Practice new words and language when talking to guests.

14. BEATEN, BATTERED, BOTTOM 80 BIKES

It's no wonder that so many stylists struggle with achieving greater financial success. They've been riding beaten, battered, Bottom 80 bikes! In some cases they have a battered back wheel with old and outdated Technical Skills. In other cases their front wheel is blown out because of little or no Guest Communication Skills. Achieving sudden and dramatic jumps in take-home pay is extremely difficult for stylists with a beaten, battered, Bottom 80 bike, because they're always losing guests.

Stylists stuck in Bottom 80 are unaware that the bicycle they've been riding on is beaten, battered, and in need of a complete update.

Anytime anyone offers them a suggestion that would improve their back wheel, like attending technical or product knowledge training, they stubbornly reject that suggestion by saying, "Leave me alone, I've been to all that training already." **What stylists stuck in Bottom 80 haven't realized is that there is a major difference between attending a class and actually applying what they learn from that class.**

TIME FOR ACTION!

1. How can a beaten and battered back wheel cause you trouble?

2. How does a beaten and battered front wheel steer you off track?

3. Draw a picture of how your bike currently looks.

15. FORMULA FOR SUCCESS

While back wheel Technical Skills and front wheel Guest Communication Skills individually influence our financial success, it's knowing the formula for developing and using both sets of skills together that really causes our personal income to explode.

FORMULA FOR SUCCESS

Technical Skills x Guest Communication Skills = *Financial Success*
BACK WHEEL   FRONT WHEEL

Imagine measuring our Technical Skills and Guest Communication Skills on a scale of 1–10, with 1 indicating low skills and 10 indicating high skills.

If we have a high Technical Skill of 8 and a low Guest Communication Skill of 2, our Financial Success Number would be only 16.

8 x 2 = 16

The reverse is also true. If we have a low Technical Skill of 2 and a high Guest Communication Skill of 8, our Financial Success Number still would be only 16.

2 x 8 = 16

But look what happens when we bring both our Technical and our Guest Communication Skills up to an 8. All of a sudden our financial success dramatically jumps to 64, which means we earn four times more money than we did when we were at 16!

$$8 \times 8 = 64$$

The **Formula for Success** gives us a deeper understanding of why Top 20s make more money. Using this formula gives us the keen awareness to see our own strengths and weaknesses in these two areas. **"What you can see you can improve."** This new awareness empowers us to identify those areas in which we must become well trained and highly skilled.

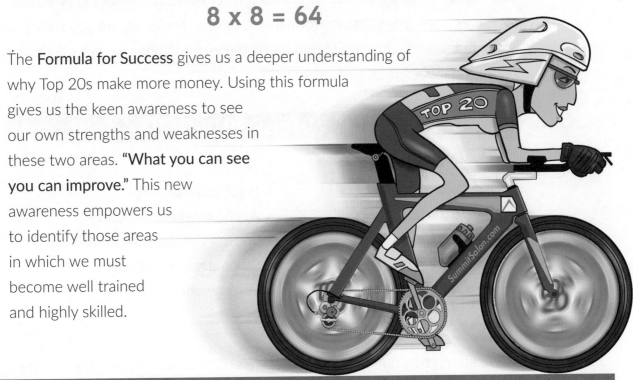

TIME FOR ACTION!

1. On a scale of 1–10, rate your current Technical Skills.

☐ ☐ ☐ ☐ ☐ ☐ ☐ ☐ ☐ ☐
1   2   3   4   5   6   7   8   9   10

2. On a scale of 1–10, rate your current Guest Communication Skills.

☐ ☐ ☐ ☐ ☐ ☐ ☐ ☐ ☐ ☐
1   2   3   4   5   6   7   8   9   10

3. Use the Formula for Success to find your current Financial Success number.

_____ x _____ = _____

Technical Skills x **Guest Communication Skills** = *Financial Success*
BACK WHEEL   FRONT WHEEL

16. BUILDING A STRONGER BACK WHEEL

We all know that Technical Skills are the techniques we use to create great looks on our guests. However there are other technical areas of our business that require us to be skillful, such as product knowledge, time management, computer knowledge, and performance tracking. Never before has having a wider range of Technical Skills in all of these areas been so critical to our greater financial success as stylists.

BACK WHEEL BUILDERS

- *Cut and Design*
- *Color*
- *Texturizing*
- *Relaxing*
- *Treatments*
- *Finishing and Styling*

- *Tools*
- *Product Knowledge*
- *Appointment Scheduling*
- *Station Set Up, Merchandising*
- *Computer Technology*
- *Performance Tracking*

As we strengthen our Technical Skills, we automatically expand the range of looks we can offer to our guests AND we gain much greater self-confidence and courage.

17. BUILDING A STRONGER FRONT WHEEL

Many of us have invested a lot of time and money into developing our Technical Skills. That's a good thing and we must continue our training. But, if we're serious about achieving sudden and dramatic jumps in our personal income, we must also put much more of our time and money into using the Power Wheel to build our front wheel/Guest Communication Skills. Just as the rider's ability to direct the bicycle with the front wheel determines the ultimate destination, our Guest Communication Skills will always determine the ultimate destination of our take-home pay.

FRONT WHEEL BUILDERS

- *Getting Guests to Like, Trust, and Respect Us*
- *Having Comfortable Social Conversations with Guests*
- *Convincing Guests to Buy Services and Products*
- *Finding Great Looks for Guests*
- *Asking Key Questions*
- *Listening and Suggesting*

- *Using Descriptive Words when Offering Looks, Services, and Products*
- *Hearing and Understanding What Guests Want*
- *Showing and Telling Guests What Products to Use*
- *Creating a Plan for each Guest's Future Visits*
- *Being Calm and Graceful with Hard-to-Please Guests*

POWER WHEEL SUMMARY

The Power Wheel is a step-by-step process, which, if practiced daily, leads to lightning-fast clientele development and financial explosions in take-home pay. Long-term and sustainable success does not happen by chance nor is it luck-of- the-draw. It happens as a result of our willingness to become highly skilled in all aspects of guest communication. **Accomplishing the success of a Top 20 demands that we give as much attention to developing the Guest Communication Skills of our front wheel as we do to the Technical Skills of our back wheel.**

BUILDING YOUR POWER WHEELS

1. Choose a skill from the **BACK WHEEL BUILDERS** list (page 46) that you want to improve.

2. How would improving that skill impact your business?

3. Choose a skill from the **FRONT WHEEL BUILDERS** list (page 47) that you want to strengthen.

4. How would strengthening that skill impact your business?

POWER WHEEL PLANNING

Top 20 Star Power

Our emotional energy has an enormous influence on the experience our guests have when they're sitting in our chair. Guests love buying services and products from stylists who radiate *Top 20 Star Power*. The more positive our energy, the more money our guests are willing to spend and the greater the explosion in our take-home pay! Nothing turns off the willingness of a guest to spend faster than the negative energy of Bottom 80. In other words the power of our own emotional energy is *always* either *making us* or *costing us* A LOT of money. For that reason we must make developing *Top 20 Star Power* as important as learning to do great hair.

KEY POINTS

- Star Power
- Top Self & Bottom Self
- See-Feel-Do-Get
- Living & Visiting
- The Remarkable Process of "NCT"
- Triggers & Indicators

- Thought Circles
- Tornadoes
- Negative Self Talk The Bad I & Good I
- Star Qualities

4 WHAT'S THE DIFFERENCE BETWEEN...

The biggest difference between a good day and a bad day is all about how much of our *Top 20 Star Power* is coming through.

1. **TOP 20 STAR POWER**

At the center of The Power Wheel is the Top 20 Star that represents the unlimited positive energy we all possess called **Star Power**. It's made up of the **positive thoughts, beliefs, attitudes, and feelings** we have about ourselves. Top 20 Star Power is another name for our **Top Self.** As we become more aware of our Star Power, our self image improves and we feel Greater Self-Esteem, Self-Worth, and Self-Confidence.

Successful stylists give lots of attention to growing their Star Power because they understand the critical link between the feelings they have about themselves and how those feelings affect everyone around them, especially the guests they serve.

As we learn how to **turn on, turn up, and turn loose** the Positive Energy of our Star Power, we become a great asset to everyone around us. We become an energizer, an encourager. We unleash a remarkable ability to inspire positive change. We bring new life to any relationship in which we're involved. The enthusiasm, joy, and light-heartedness we radiate attract good things to us and everyone around us. **We become more of our Top Self.**

2. OVER & UNDER THE LINE

The illustration below is a simple model we can use as a tool to grow and develop our Star Power. The vertical line going up and down is a yardstick we use to measure the quality and usefulness of our thinking. The higher up we go into our **BLUE** Top Self or **TS**, the clearer, more positive, and useful our thoughts and beliefs become. **This is Top 20 Thinking.** The lower we go into our **RED** Bottom 80 Self or **BS**, the gloomier, more negative, and useless our thoughts and beliefs are. **This is Bottom 80 Thinking.**

On this same model there is a horizontal line going directly out from the yardstick. This separates Top 20 Thinking from Bottom 80 Thinking. This line is simply called the **Line**. When we're **Over the Line** our thinking is working for us much better than it is when we're **Under the Line**.

All of us fluctuate between being Over and Under the Line. It's perfectly normal to have highs and lows. But, if we want to bring out more of our Top Self and our Star Power Qualities, **we must become skillful at recognizing and overcoming our RED Bottom 80 thinking.**

TS: TOP 20 SELF
Our thoughts are clear, positive, and useful

BS: BOTTOM 80 SELF
Our thoughts are gloomy, negative, and useless

3. THE FRAME

This next illustration is called the **Frame** and it gives us a simple explanation of the powerful role Top 20 and Bottom 80 Thinking plays in determining our financial success and the overall quality of our life.

Developing the Star Power of our Top Self is all about knowing that our **THINKING** is connected to what we **SEE**, what we **FEEL**, what we **DO** and what we **GET**. Here's how the process works:

- Our **THINKING** determines what we **SEE**.
- What we SEE determines how we **FEEL**.
- How we FEEL determines what we **DO**.
- What we DO determines what we **GET**.

4. TOP 20/BOTTOM 80 FRAME

When we combine Over and Under the Line with the Frame, we have a better understanding of what happens to our thinking when we fall Under the Line to Bottom 80, or jump Over the Line to Top 20.

When we are Over the Line, our thinking is **Top 20 BLUE**—we see and feel positive about ourselves, we respond by doing positive things and, as a result, we get a prosperous career and an extraordinary life.

The opposite is also true. Whenever we're Under the Line, our thinking automatically goes to **Bottom 80 RED**—we SEE and FEEL negative about ourselves and our life, we react by DOing negative things. As a result, we GET a troubled life filled with chaos, drama, and scarcity.

An example of how this plays out is found on the next page.

WHEN WE ARE OVER THE LINE IN TOP 20

We **SEE** ourselves as being intelligent and creative. We have an optimistic point of view and believe we are worthy of having a better life.

We **FEEL** greater Self-Esteem, Self-Confidence, and Self-Worth. Our emotions are filled with positive energy.

We **GET** a life of personal fulfillment, greater well being, healthy relationships, and tremendous wealth.

We **DO** things to take better care of ourselves, our relationships, and our personal and professional finances.

WHEN WE ARE UNDER THE LINE IN BOTTOM 80

We **SEE** ourselves as being stupid and not as good as other people. We have a pessimistic point of view, and believe we are unworthy of having a better life.

We **FEEL** overwhelmed, depressed, angry, annoyed, and worried. Our emotions are charged with negative energy.

We **GET** a life full of personal drama, troubled relationships, and financial set backs.

We **DO** things that sabotage ourselves, our relationships, and our personal and professional finances.

TIME FOR ACTION!

1. How would your life be different if more of your Top 20 Star Power was coming through?

2. How do you see yourself when you are Over the Line in TS?

3. How do you see yourself when you are Under the Line in BS?

5. LIVING AND VISITING

Being Over or Under the Line isn't a good thing or a bad thing—it's a human thing. But there is a big difference between living in **BLUE** Top Self (TS) and visiting **RED** Bottom Self (BS), as opposed to living in BS and visiting TS.

Visiting BS is normal, but where we're at most of the time is where we live. If our thinking is clear and positive most of the time, we *live* in TS and *visit* BS.

On the other hand if our thinking is mostly gloomy and negative, chances are pretty good that we *live* in BS and *visit* TS.

The key to tapping into the positive energy of our Top 20 Star Power is to develop the awareness and skill to live in TS even when conditions aren't favorable.

LIVE IN Top Self (TS) and visit Bottom Self (BS)

LIVE IN Bottom Self (BS) and visit Top Self (TS)

6. **THE REMARKABLE PROCESS OF "NCT"**

We can use the remarkable process of NCT to break out of Living in Bottom 80 and move into Top 20. Practicing the process of NCT enables us to further develop the Star Power of our Top Self. NCT is made of three crucial parts: **Name, Claim, and Tame**. While each part has its own unique purpose, when all three parts are working as one, they become an amazing force of positive change.

NAME

Naming is about having the awareness to see our own negative thinking and realizing how it's getting in the way of our greater success. Naming is the ability to see when we're in BS. **What we can see, we can control. What we can't see, controls us.** Naming our negative thoughts, feelings, and behaviors means waking up and getting honest with ourselves. Whatever we can name, we can change. Most of our ability to break out of BS comes from having the courage to NAME it. The moment we **NAME** our BS habits, the remarkable process of NCT is set in motion and begins changing us for the better.

CLAIM

Claiming is about accepting personal responsibility for changing our thoughts, feelings, and behaviors without blaming others or shaming ourselves. What we accept personal responsibility for, we can change for the better. To blame is to deny responsibility for being in our BS or rationalize it by finding fault with others, then blasting them for upsetting us.

To shame is to beat ourselves up for the mistakes and messes we've made. **Nothing ruins our success faster than blaming and shaming.** We must realize that dropping into BS comes with life, and that it isn't necessary to blame others or shame ourselves. We can use Claiming to bypass blaming and shaming and go right to Taming.

TAME

Taming is all about the actions we must take to breakout of our BS. While Naming and Claiming are important, they are useless unless we are willing to make the commitment to taking those actions until they become a habit. What we take action on, we can change for good.

Studies tell us that it takes 21 days of new actions to change a habit. **The self-defeating habits of our Bottom Self require at least 21 days of taming actions to change them.**

NCT AT A GLANCE

NAME: The moment we name our BS habits (judgment, worrying, stubbornness, gossiping, etc.), the remarkable process of NCT is set in motion and begins changing us for the better.

CLAIM: We don't have to make anyone wrong before making something right. We don't have to make ourselves (or anyone else) bad before making something better. **We must accept personal responsibility for the BS habits that we want to tame.** This allows us to bypass blaming and shaming and go right to Taming.

TAME: We will never be able to change our habits unless we are willing to take action to do so. The good news is that *Over The Top* is filled with great Taming actions. Don't hesitate to take action. Even small changes can make enormous differences.

7. TRIGGERS AND INDICATORS

Having an awareness of what can Trigger our BS is an important part of naming, claiming, and taming it. **Triggers** are those situations or persons that activate negative thoughts, feelings, and behaviors. Think of the last time you were having a good day, and something happened that made you immediately start thinking, feeling, and reacting in negative ways. That thing that happened is probably a Trigger of yours. When we react negatively to a Trigger, we empower it to control us.

Along with Triggers we must use our awareness to see what our Indicators are. **Indicators** are feelings or reactions that tell us we have dropped into BS. Using the process of NCT to name, claim, and tame our Triggers and Indicators is a giant step towards breaking out of our BS and enjoying greater financial success.

TRIGGERS

- *Somebody Calling You Stupid*
- *Somebody Laughing at You*
- *Running Behind*
- *No Shows*
- *Slow Week*
- *Mean and Rude Guests*

INDICATORS

- *Feelings: anger, frustration, sadness, jealousy, depression, worry, panic*
- *Reactions: yelling, fighting, arguing, complaining, criticizing, shutting down, giving up, crying, melting down*

TIME FOR ACTION!

1. What does it feel like to live in Bottom 80?

2. What does it feel like to live in Top 20?

3. Bring to mind a bad habit you are willing to NAME, CLAIM, and TAME.

   a. *NAME the habit.* _____

   b. *Describe how you will CLAIM personal responsibility for this habit.*

   c. *Describe the COURAGEOUS actions you will take to TAME it.*

4. What Triggers your BS?

5. What are some Indicators that your BS has been Triggered?

   a. *How do you feel?*

   b. *What do you say?*

   c. *How do you act?*

6. How is your BS keeping you from making more money?

8. NEGATIVE THOUGHT CIRCLES

Negative Thought Circles are self-defeating thinking habits that plague us when we drop into BS. A **Thought Circle** is always triggered by one negative thought which leads to another negative thought and another and another, like a snowball getting larger and larger as it rolls down a hill. As our Thought Circle gets bigger and bigger with each negative thought, we take a nose dive deeper and deeper into BS.

Thought Circles get triggered when it sounds like guests don't like, trust, or respect us. They may ask us a question like: **"So, how long have you been in the business?"** We immediately jump to conclusions, make ourselves nervous, lose our self-confidence, and become overwhelmed, all because of one question. And our Thought Circle is off and running.

We freak ourselves out by our own negative Thought Circles and sabotage our credibility with guests. As a result we treat them in ways that make them dislike us, ruining our chance of getting them to come back.

I have to get her out of here NOW!

She'll hate what I do and not come back.

...and doesn't think I know what I'm doing!

She obviously doesn't like me...

HOW RUDE!

SO.... How long have you been in the business?

9. NAMING, CLAIMING, AND TAMING NEGATIVE THOUGHT CIRCLES

The best way to break up negative Thought Circles is to get better at naming, claiming, and taming them. The sooner we can catch ourselves in a negative thought circle, the easier it is to stop it. A simple way to stop them is to use the "STOP! NOT NOW" technique. **Whenever we catch ourselves beginning a negative Thought Circle, think:** *"Stop! This is a Thought Circle. Not Now."*

As we get better at breaking up negative Thought Circles, more of our Star Power shines through. Our full attention then goes to the person in front of us, which brings more good into our lives.

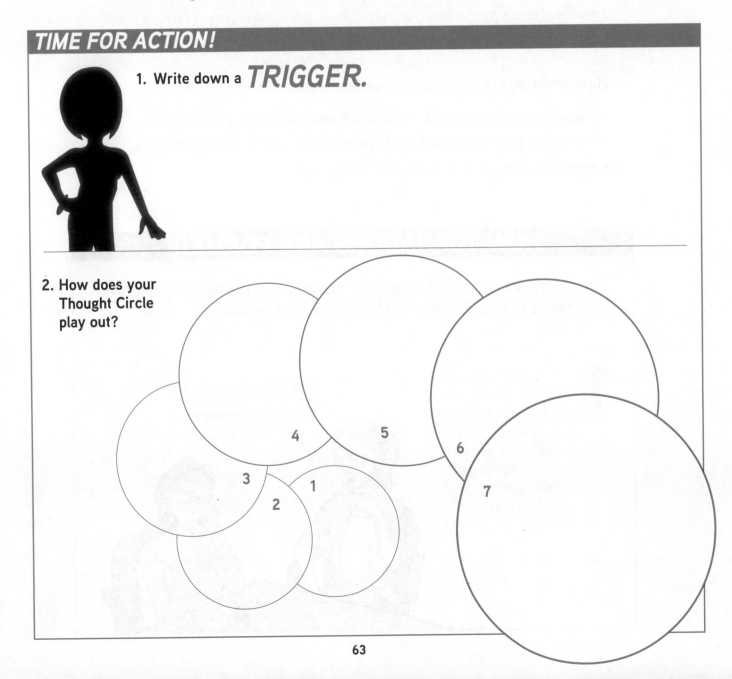

TIME FOR ACTION!

1. **Write down a** *TRIGGER.*

2. **How does your Thought Circle play out?**

4 5 6 3 1 2 7

10. **TORNADOES**

Have you ever seen a tornado movie? There's always a cow, a fence, and a pick-up truck flying across the road. The destructive force of a tornado occurs because of its tremendous energy. It wreaks havoc on everything in its path. In the salon, when someone is in the midst of a BS Thought Circle, they can easily start complaining to those around them.

A common reaction to someone else's complaining is to agree with it and then add our own complaining. This kind of reaction usually comes from a need to be supported, liked, and accepted by others. A tornado begins to form and the destructive energy has the power to draw innocent bystanders into the emotional chaos and drama. Tornadoes have tremendous power to negatively influence an entire group and their culture.

How individual and group influence works:

• A <u>positive person or group</u> tends to influence others in <u>positive ways</u>.

• A <u>negative person or group</u> tends to influence others in <u>negative ways</u>.

• *Energy is contagious. Be careful what you catch!*

HOW TORNADOES ARE FORMED

Tornadoes are easily and quickly formed because the negative energy unleashed from a Thought Circle is highly contagious.

1. Whenever a negative Thought Circle has us disturbed, we have a need to talk about it with other people in an attempt to get their agreement and support.

They're out of their mind if they think I'm going to that stupid training program on my day off.

HOW TORNADOES ARE FORMED (continued)

2. As soon as another person gets drawn into the conversation, a Tornado is spawned.

3. The Tornado's negative energy now has the power to pull a third or fourth unsuspecting individual into the emotional drama. As this happens, the negative energy gets more and more intense and tends to dominate the entire group culture, putting everyone in a bad MOOoood!!

11. NAMING, CLAIMING, & TAMING TORNADOES

The process of NCT can help us in two ways. It helps us avoid getting dragged into a tornado and it also helps us break the destructive BS habit of being a tornado starter.

TORNADO WATCH:
Know where conditions are right for producing Tornadoes.
Be aware of where Tornadoes can occur: Backroom, Front Desk, Outside of Salon, at a Bar, Coffee Shop, or Restaurant, or on Cell Phones, in Texts, and in Emails

TORNADO WARNING:
A funnel cloud has actually been sighted.
Indicators that a Tornado is forming: Complaining, Criticizing, Nit-Picking, Arguing, Blaming, Fault Finding, Backbiting, Badmouthing, Gossiping

TORNADO TOUCHDOWN:
The twister has hit the ground.
Before you know it you are in it, and have become, an active participant.

NAMING TORNADOES

Sometimes we find ourselves in the middle of a swirling Tornado without even knowing how we got there. Therefore we must develop the awareness to identify Tornadoes quickly to avoid being pulled into them. Whenever approaching a group where it looks and sounds like a Tornado is being spawned, say to yourself, "Uh oh, it looks like a Tornado is going on over there. I better watch out."

Getting better at spotting Tornadoes before we walk into them empowers us with the ability to protect ourselves from their destructive energy. Just as they do on a weather channel, it's important that we pay attention to Tornado watches, warnings, and touchdowns.

CLAIMING TORNADOES

Claiming is about accepting personal responsibility for either starting Tornadoes or adding our negative energy to an existing Tornado. Accepting personal responsibility for our part in Tornadoes without shaming ourselves or blaming others, empowers us to change for the better.

TAMING TORNADOES

The following are Taming actions we must become skillful at in order to protect ourselves from Tornadoes.

• LISTEN WITHOUT AGREEING OR JUDGING

There is a big difference between agreeing or disagreeing with another person's emotional drama and just listening to it with no need to jump in with opinions or judgments. The minute we join the conversation with our opinions, we get pulled into the swirl. **It is possible to listen without agreeing or disagreeing.**

• RESPOND BY SAYING, "I HEAR YOU."

Sometimes engaging in Tornadoes is the social activity in groups we hang out with. In those situations many of us feel the pressure to either participate or run the risk of being the subject of ridicule and rejection. Somebody caught in a Tornado might attempt to pull us into the drama by saying, "So, what do you think?" A safe and effective response is to say simply, "I hear you."

By saying, "I hear you," we are acknowledging what another person is experiencing without being drawn into the Tornado ourselves. We can observe the Tornado and not be damaged by it or harm others.

• LEAVE THE TORNADO SCENE

"I hear you," is a highly effective response to a Tornado. However, if the Tornado persists with its "seek and destroy" mission, we may need to repeat, "I hear you," a second time or simply get up and walk away.

• STOP BEING A TORNADO STARTER

We can easily develop a reputation of being a Tornado starter. It becomes part of our identity within our group and people come to expect it from us. While it may appear to gain us status within the group, in the long run, it is self-destructive, keeps our Star Power from developing, and sabotages our success. This is why it's important to break the BS habit of being a Tornado starter.

TAMING TORNADOES (CONTINUED)

• TAKE MORE DRASTIC MEASURES

Tornadoes are extremely dangerous. If certain friends or the group we hang out with are dominated by Tornadoes, we may need to take more drastic measures to protect ourselves. We can do this by **expanding** our social circle, **limiting** our time with Tornado-dominated groups, or **terminating** some relationships.

EXPAND YOUR SOCIAL CIRCLE: The more friends we have and groups we are associated with, the less influence any individual or particular group will have on us. Having a bigger social circle always gives us more options.

Ideas and suggestions for expanding your social circle

- *Get involved in new activities.*
- *Make good impressions on peers or classmates.*
- *Step outside your comfort zone by setting a goal to meet new people.*
- *Don't worry about Other People's Opinions of you.*

LIMIT OUR TIME: If certain friends in our lives are having too much negative influence on us, we can limit the time we spend with them. A good way of limiting our availability is by making other plans.

TERMINATE THE RELATIONSHIP: Sometimes it is necessary to actually end the relationship. When is it time to end it? We may have tried talking about the problem, or we may have tried being a positive influence, but it's not getting any better. If this relationship continues to drag us into Tornadoes, it may be time to terminate it. Whenever a relationship is influencing us in a negative direction consider ending the relationship.

12. NCT: A POWER GREATER THAN TORNADOES

Naming, Claiming, and Taming our Tornadoes does not mean that we should never share our negative feelings with family or friends. We can get perspective and help when we share our feelings and concerns in a healthy way. This is very different from only wanting to complain.

Using the remarkable process of NCT to Name, Claim, and Tame Tornadoes empowers us with the Star Power to have better relationships and a more successful career.

TIME FOR ACTION!

1. **Where in your life do Tornadoes start to form?**

2. **When do you find yourself starting Tornadoes?**

3. **Bring to mind the last Tornado you found yourself in. Which one of the Taming Actions would have helped?**

4. **Consider the negative influences in your social life. Do you need to:**

   a. *EXPAND your friendships?*

   b. *LIMIT your time with someone?*

   c. *TERMINATE a relationship?*

13. NEGATIVE SELF-TALK

There are times when we fall into BS, lose our confidence, and get filled with doubt. We become afraid that we don't have the strength or intelligence to make our dreams come true, and we start thinking or saying negative things about ourselves. "I am never going to be able to learn to do this. I am not as good as the rest of the people here."

Many of us have the BS habit of negative self-talk, which is a defeating tendency of thinking and talking about ourselves negatively. This BS habit keeps us stuck in Bottom 80 and is a major obstacle to discovering and developing our Top 20 Star Power. The Frame gives us a keen awareness of the destructive force of negative self talk. If we want greater success in our life we must break the habit of negative self-talk.

BOTTOM 80 NEGATIVE SELF-TALK		
When I **SEE** myself as not being good enough.		I **FEEL** depressed, annoyed, or overwhelmed
I **GET** a life that is increasingly miserable.		I **DO** myself harm by thinking and talking negatively about myself.

14. NAMING, CLAIMING, & TAMING NEGATIVE SELF-TALK

Once again we can use the process of NCT to help us break the BS habit of thinking and talking about ourselves in ways that limit our success.

NAMING NEGATIVE SELF-TALK

RECOGNIZING THE BAD **I**

The most important letter in the alphabet is the letter **I** because **whatever we say after we say I is what we become.** Therefore the first thing we must do to stop negative self talk is to become aware of the BAD **I**. Any time the letter **I** is followed by a negative statement, we are using the BAD **I**. To break the habit of negative self-talk we must develop the awareness to see when we are using it. While there are different kinds of BAD **I**s, they all have one thing in common: they keep us from feeling good and having a great life. Getting skillful at identifying when we are using a BAD **I** empowers us to stop its destructive force. Some of the BAD **I**s to watch out for include: **ANGRY BAD I**, **DEPRESSED BAD I**, and **WORRIED BAD I**.

THE BAD **I**

"I am not as good as the rest of the people here."

"I just can't stay focused."

"I am never going to be able to do this."

"I have tried stuff like this before and I just couldn't do it."

"I am not smart enough."

"I am so stupid."

"I guess that's just the way I AM."

"I am the only one who does anything around here and I am sick of it."

CLAIMING NEGATIVE SELF-TALK

Claiming negative self-talk is about admitting that we get in our own way of progress more than anyone else by belittling everything about ourselves. Accepting responsibility for changing our own negative self-talk unleashes the power in us to change it for the better.

TAMING NEGATIVE SELF-TALK

BELIEVING IN THE GOOD I

All it takes to start taming is **ONE GOOD I**. Many of us have been harshly criticized by others and led to believe we are not good enough, smart enough, strong enough, nor worthy enough to have an extraordinary life. Consequently we end up spending far too much time feeling badly about who we are, denying or devaluing our talents, achievements, or desires, and becoming extremely hard on ourselves.

The truth is we are good enough, smart enough, strong enough, and worthy enough to have an extraordinary life. This is our True Self or our **GOOD I**. The sooner we STOP believing in the lies of the **BAD I** and START believing in and acknowledging our **GOOD I**, the more empowered we become to change for the better and have a greater life.

THE GOOD I

"I deserve a good life."

"I have more than enough intelligence."

"I am willing, able, and worthy of greater wealth."

"I can learn how to do this."

"I have talent." "I like myself."

"I have the strength I need to get through this."

"I will get through this."

15. STOP LISTENING TO NEGATIVE OPOs

Many of our **BAD I**s have come from negative OPOs, **O**ther **P**eople's **O**pinions of us. Stylists stuck in Bottom 80 think OPOs are so important they are willing to let them determine their actions. It's important to be open to feedback because it can help us grow. When feedback is filled with negative opinions and judgments, we need to remind ourselves that: <u>OPOs</u> **of us are none of our business.** There's nothing more vital to our emotional and financial health than to ignore, disregard, and detach from the OPOs of those hell-bent on getting us to believe that we lack the intelligence and strength to have an extraordinary life. Instead, we must believe in our GOOD **I**, and hang out with people who will encourage us with Positive Energy.

The best way to break the grip of OPOs is to drop our negative opinions of ourselves and the negative opinions we have of others. **The *only opinion* we should concern ourselves with is the GOOD opinion we have of ourselves and of others.** As we stop judging ourselves, other people, and those who judge us, we will be less concerned with what other people are thinking about us and more interested in expressing our Star Power in extraordinary ways that make our lives better.

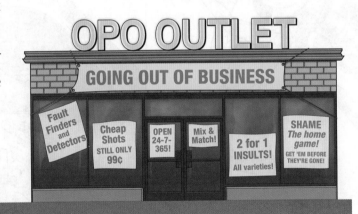

TIME FOR ACTION!

1. **Write down a BAD I you have said about yourself (page 71).**

2. **Write down a negative OPO that I need to make "none of my business."**

3. **Write down a GOOD I that would help you to overcome this BAD I and/or negative OPO.**

BOTTOM 80 POWER POPPERS

STORM STARTER

Never misses an opportunity to start an emotional tornado by spreading negative energy throughout the salon.

STORM CHASER

Would NEVER start a tornado, but can't resist the lure to participate in the emotional drama and chaos of a tornado.

RUNAWAY BRAIN

Staying awake all night long worrying about problems. Believing that the light at the end of the tunnel is actually a train coming our way.

OPO COLLECTOR

Have a wide collection of negative OPOs and are influenced by OPOs.

The following are common examples of how we pop opportunities for greater income when we fall into Bottom 80 Star Power.

CYCLOPS

A negative point of view that only sees what's wrong, bad, or incorrect.

QUEEN OF BS

Has all the dirt on everybody and uses the power of drama to rule over the kingdom of BS.

STAR POWER POLICE

Those who think that it's their job to point out who's in Top 20 and who's stuck in Bottom 80.

TIME FOR ACTION!

1. Identify those Power Poppers you can relate to most.

2. How does the one you chose pop opportunities for building your Star Power?

16. STAR QUALITIES

Getting skillful at the process of NCT empowers us to break out of BS by:

- *Stopping Thought Circles sooner*
- *Watching out for and protecting ourselves from Tornadoes*
- *Overcoming the habit of negative self-talk*
- *Not listening to OPOs*

If we are serious about achieving dramatic and sudden increases in our personal income, we must be absolutely willing to show more of our Top Self by developing more of our Star Power. As we begin making these changes, more of our Top 20 Star Power bursts forth and is revealed and developed into positive characteristics called STAR QUALITIES.

EMOTIONAL AWARENESS
in touch with feelings and thoughts

FOCUSED
on work at hand

ASSERTIVE
confident and direct

ENTHUSIASTIC
lively interest

COURAGEOUS
responding in spite of fear

ORGANIZED
able to keep our life in order

OPTIMISTIC
hopeful, seeing the positive

PERSISTENT
stick with it

STAR QUALITIES

CREATIVE
inventive, full of ideas

OUTGOING
friendly, sociable

PROACTIVE
doing what needs to be done before a problem develops

RESPONSIBLE
willing to be accountable

SELF-CONFIDENT
belief in oneself

SELF-MOTIVATED
self-starting

RESILIENT
able to bounce back quickly after a set back

SELF-DISCIPLINED
having self-control

TOP 20 STAR POWER SUMMARY

Star Power is the **positive thoughts, beliefs, attitudes, and feelings** we have about ourselves. And, it has an enormous influence on the experience our guests have with us. Our Star Power is the number one predictor of our greater financial success or failure because the quality of our emotional energy influences every part of our life. Contrary to popular belief, our Star Power can be developed and our negative self-defeating habits can be overcome.

As we discover and develop the Positive Energy of our Star Power, every aspect of our life explodes in prosperous and remarkable ways. We become an inspiration to everyone around us and a vision of what's possible when people have the willingness to step up and change for the better. **We become Top 20!**

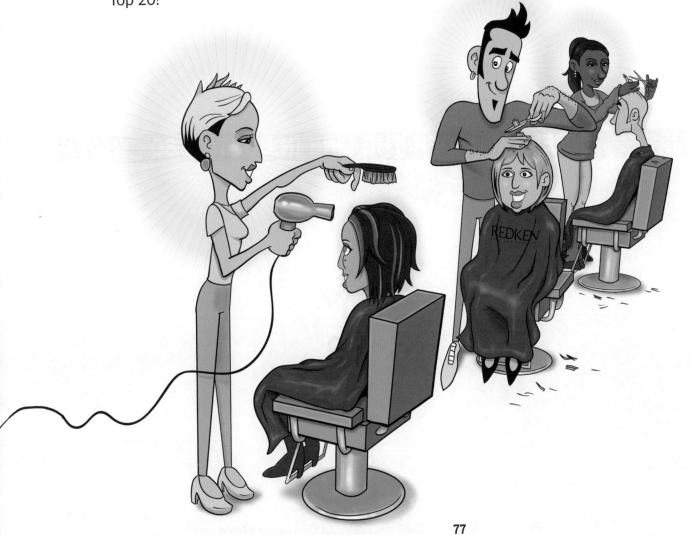

OVER & UNDER THE LINE FRAME EXERCISE

Fill in the Frame about yourself when you are Over the Line in TS and Under the Line in BS.

- *How do you SEE yourself?* • *How does that seeing make you FEEL?*
- *When you feel that way what do you DO, say, and how do you act?*
- *What do you end up GETTING when you SEE, FEEL, and DO in TS and BS?*

WHEN I'M OVER THE LINE IN TOP 20

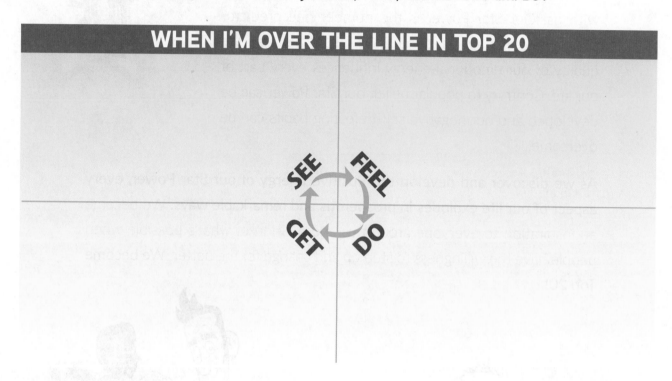

WHEN I'M UNDER THE LINE IN BOTTOM 80

POSITIVE "GOOD I" WORKSHEET

1. Write some GOOD Is about your coworkers.

2. Write some GOOD Is about yourself.

TOP 20 STAR QUALITIES WORKSHEET

1. What are the Star Qualities you want more of?

Bonding

Gaining credibility quickly with guests is a major factor in achieving dramatic and sudden jumps in personal income. Bonding is our first real opportunity to start building credibility by making positive and lasting first impressions. Positive first impressions make our guests feel great about the money they are going to be spending on our services and products, which leads to more repeat and referral business. This is why becoming highly skilled at Top 20 Bonding is so important.

KEY POINTS

- Bonding Defined
- Reducing Guest Tension
- High Anxiety
- First Impressions
- Guest Communication
- Three Ways to Communicate
- Yes Momentum
- Giving Direction
- Four Steps to a Top 20 Greeting

5 HAVE YOU EVER GONE OUT...

...and been freaked out by what you saw?

REMEMBER: Guests judge us as quickly as we judge them.
How you handle this relationship is called *Top 20 Bonding*.

1. BONDING

Bonding is the first step of the Power Wheel and is best defined as building credibility and rapport with our guests. **Credibility and rapport is the ability to get our guests to like, trust, and respect us.** Bonding is the process of taking a sometimes anxious, fearful, belligerent, or confused guest and creating confidence in that guest that we know what we're doing. Through the process of Bonding, the guest learns to feel safe, comfortable, and trusting. The credibility and rapport we develop with a guest will lead to more sales, rebooks, and referrals, as well as making the guest feel better about the time and money spent with us. Bonding plays a much bigger role in building a full book because guests don't return to stylists whom they don't like, trust, or respect.

2. THE FRAME AND BONDING

The quality of the attitude and feelings we have as we meet and greet our guests will determine how successful we are at Bonding with them. When we are in Top 20 **BLUE** and the Positive Energy of our Star Power is coming through us, our guests pick up on our enthusiasm and the Bonding process gets off to an excellent start.

But when we drop into Bottom 80 **RED** and the negative energy of our BS comes through, we become self-centered, judgmental, unable to establish credibility, and our chances of Bonding go out the window.

IN BOTTOM 80 BS WE		IN TOP 20 STAR POWER WE	
SEE Bonding with guests as unimportant, and take new guests for granted.	**FEEL** indifferent, uncaring, disinterested, or annoyed.	**SEE** Bonding with guests as an important part of developing a great clientele.	**FEEL** a genuine sense of interest, care, and concern for our guests.
GET disappointed guests who don't spend their money because they don't like, trust, or respect us.	**DO** poorly at building credibility and rapport.	**GET** guests who are willing to spend more money because they like, trust, and respect us.	**DO** a great job at building credibility and rapport by treating guests in a warm and friendly way.

TIME FOR ACTION!

LIKE	**TRUST**	**RESPECT**
When the guest finds us enjoyable to be around.	When guests believe we have their best interest at heart.	When the guest believes we know what we're doing.

1. Which of the three parts of Bonding are you best at? LIKE   TRUST RESPECT

2. Which of the three do you want your guests to give you more of? LIKE TRUST RESPECT

3. What's your Greeting like when you're in Bottom 80 BS?

3. FIRST IMPRESSIONS

Whenever we go to see a doctor or dentist for the first time we experience a certain amount of tension. Now imagine what it's like for a new guest meeting us for the first time. Many guests have learned the hard way that we have the power to drastically alter how they look and feel. This is why they want to know that they will be safe in our hands.

Whether we're aware of it or not, the moment we come into contact with our guest we are making a first impression. That first impression can be either a positive or negative one. Positive impressions cause prosperous results, while negative impressions cause disastrous results.

When we make negative first impressions, guest tension goes up and it takes a mountain of time and energy to reduce it.

But when the impressions we make are positive, guest tension is quickly reduced, we bond with them, and they begin taking direction from us. Guess how long it takes to make a first impression? If you said ten seconds, you're absolutely right. Ten seconds from the time guests see us, they have an impression of who we are.

4. NEW GUEST TENSION

As new guests arrive, they are naturally nervous. A Top 20 Attitude gives us the power to put guests at ease, while a Bottom 80 Attitude sends them into a state of panic.

The **Vertical Line** illustrates the level of tension new guests are feeling. At the bottom, tension is low and they feel comfortable and relaxed. At the top, tension is high and guests feel nervous, anxious, or fearful.

The **Horizontal Line** tells us how many minutes a guest has been with us.

Top 20 Bonding means getting guests to like us. We do this by developing the ability to reduce their tension quickly.

Guess where most new guests are when they enter the salon?

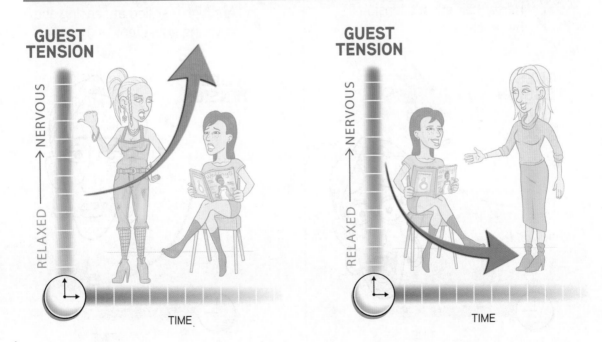

A TALE OF TWO GREETINGS

The FASTER we can get guests to RELAX, the easier it is to get them to BUY OUR SERVICES AND PRODUCTS because guests hear us better when they are relaxed.

5. HIGH ANXIETY

Stylists stuck in Bottom 80 are untrained in Bonding and as a result are unaware of the fears that first-time guests experience. Consequently they are unskilled at reducing guest tension, and many times they make it worse. Most new guests come in nervous, and after a few seconds with a Bottom 80 Bonder, their anxiety goes through the roof. When our guest's tension is high, they can't hear our great ideas because they are unable to relax.

80/20 GUEST TENSION COMPARISONS

BOTTOM 80	TOP 20
▶ Are unaware of guest tension and think the problem is about getting "difficult guests."	▶ Are keenly aware of the tension that new guests experience.
▶ Are filled with their own anxiety about serving new guests.	▶ Stay calm and positive when faced with guest tension.
▶ Take no responsibility for the guest being difficult.	▶ Know that it's their responsibility to lower guest tension.
▶ Raise their guest's tension by reacting to it.	▶ Are highly skilled at sensing and lowering guest tension quickly.

GUEST TENSION

NERVOUS ← → RELAXED

TIME

GUEST TENSION

NERVOUS ← → RELAXED

TIME

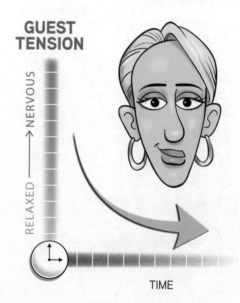

6. THE #1 CREDIBILITY KILLER

Just as guests can have negative judgments of us from the impressions we make, we can have negative judgments of them. And nothing kills our emotional energy and credibility with guests faster than our BS habit of making negative judgments about first-time guests.

How often do we go out to greet our new guests and as soon as we see them, we make one of the following judgments:

- "OH NO!"
- "Look at her, what a mess! What am I going to do with that?"
- "It's a Rug Rat...I hate doing kids, little brats never sit still!"
- "Look at that old bat. She's older than dirt. I hate old people!"
- "Look at that guy...he looks like a perve!"
- "Another coupon clipper. I get all the bargain hunters."
- "She looks like a real B****!"

We must always remember that our guests' impression of us is heavily influenced by our judgments of them. When our judgment of them is negative, they pick up on our negative energy, which causes them to have a negative impression of us. All negative judgments are highly contagious, and as our new guest catches ours, they will immediately have similar judgments of us.

TIME FOR ACTION!

1. What are some things that raise guest tension?

2. Describe a time when you made a negative first impression and your guest's tension went through the roof.

3. Describe a time when you made a positive first impression and reduced your guest's tension quickly.

4. What are some of the negative judgments you have of guests when you're in Bottom 80?

7. GUEST COMMUNICATION

Our level of skillfulness at Guest Communication will always determine how successful we are at reducing tension, making positive first impressions, and establishing credibility with guests. At first glance, this looks easy, but there's a lot more to it than meets the eye.

Did you know that **we cannot *not* communicate**? We cannot *not* impress. Even if we just stand there and say nothing, we're saying something. How can that be? What could a person just standing there being quiet possibly be saying? Any number of things, from: "I'm nervous, overwhelmed, and scared to death of you," to "I'm irritated, annoyed, and can't wait to get rid of you," to "I'm confident, friendly, and happy to meet you."

overwhelmed   ANNOYED   *CONFIDENT*

8. THREE KINDS OF GUEST COMMUNICATION

Top 20s are highly skilled in making lasting, positive impressions by using the three kinds of Guest Communication: **Verbal, Extra-Verbal, and Non-Verbal.** While all three ways combine to create Guest Communication, each one of them is effective in varying degrees. Most people tend to think of Verbal Communication as being the most effective. It seems like that's what we do most. We couldn't be more mistaken. It's just that many of us are unaware of the powerful impact created by Extra-Verbal and Non-Verbal Communication. Studies have found that Extra-Verbal and Non-Verbal Communication account for 95% of the overall impression we make. A Bottom 80 Attitude sends out Extra-Verbal and Non-Verbal signals that make one negative impression after another. Raising our awareness of these three forms of communication is essential to building credibility and Bonding with our guests.

NON-VERBAL 60%
The way we look and act.

EXTRA-VERBAL and NON-VERBAL communication make up 95% of the overall impression we make.

EXTRA-VERBAL 35%

The feeling behind the words we use.

Hi, I'm Mary! Nice to meet you.

Hi. I'm Mary.
Nice to meet you.

VERBAL 5%
The words we use.

9. VERBAL: THE WORDS WE USE

Verbal Communication makes up 5% of the impression we make. The skillful use of descriptive and exciting words that create a mental picture can quickly raise guest interest. Top 20s are always expanding and refining their vocabulary with words that are kind, friendly, and gracious, as well as great words that best describe the services and products they offer. In order to bond with guests, we must learn to create interesting conversations with purpose by choosing meaningful words that our guests understand.

80/20 VERBAL SKILLS (5%)

BOTTOM 80		TOP 20
Forget, Don't Use, Use Incorrectly	◀ GUEST'S NAME ▶	Use Correctly and Often
Slang/Vulgar Limited, Negative, Same Word Repeated, Unclear Technical Terms	◀ VOCABULARY ▶	Descriptive, Wide Range, Positive, Variety, Clear & Simple Guest-Friendly Terms
PASSIVE: Shy, Little Engagement in Conversation AGGRESSIVE: Too Much Talking About Self, Arrogant	◀ STYLE ▶	ASSERTIVE: Balanced Amount of Social with Professional Conversation

TIME FOR ACTION!

1. What are some ways to remember to use the guest's name?

2. What is your current Verbal style? Passive? Aggressive?

3. What are some ways to become more skillful at Verbal Communication?

10. EXTRA-VERBAL: THE FEELING BEHIND WORDS WE USE

Extra-Verbal Communication is about how we sound and the feelings we put into our words. Extra-Verbal makes up 35% of the impression we make, because it communicates the feelings behind the words we use. **Feelings are hard to mask and guests will always be more affected by our feelings than by our words.** Having a keen awareness of our Top 20 or Bottom 80 Attitude is so important because our feelings come from our attitude. Guests will find us enjoyable or annoying just by how our words sound and feel. Bonding with guests requires us to become highly skilled at using the sound, tone, pitch, and pace of our voice.

80/20 EXTRA-VERBAL SKILLS (35%)

Sharp, Cold, Mean, Uncertain, Nervous, Bored, Depressed, Uninterested, Non-Caring, Annoyed, Frustrated, Angry, Rude	◀ TONE ▶	Warm & Friendly, Confident & Calm, Enthusiastic, Interested, Caring, Happy
Too Loud or Soft, Too Fast or Slow, Hard to Understand	◀ PITCH & PACE ▶	Clear Tone of Voice, Even Pace, Easy to Understand

TIME FOR ACTION!

1. **SOUND & TONE: What would the following greeting sound like in a:**
   Sharp or Cold Tone • Nervous Tone • Bored Tone • Annoyed or Angry Tone

   "Hi, my name is _____ and I'll be doing your hair today."

2. **PITCH & PACE: What would the following greeting sound like:**
   Too Loud • Too Soft • Too Fast • Too Slow • Too Hard to Understand

   "Hi, my name is _____ and I'll be doing your hair today."

3. **When you're stuck in Bottom 80 what do your Extra-Verbals sound like?**

11. NON-VERBAL: THE WAY WE LOOK AND ACT

Non-Verbal Communication is a huge factor in the Bonding experience because it accounts for 60% of the impressions we make. Even though our Non-Verbal Communication is silent, it is always speaking loud and clear to our guests about who we are. And, just like Extra-Verbal Communication, our Non-Verbals send messages to our guests about our feelings. **Feelings are contagious, and guests catch our feelings from our Non-Verbal messages.** Many Top 20 stylists have unique takes on self expression and personal image. They also know that having a Top 20 Attitude of guest friendliness allows their self expression and personal image to work FOR THEM instead of against them.

80/20 NON-VERBAL SKILLS (60%)

Bottom 80		Top 20
No Smiles, No Eye Contact, Frowning	◀ **FACIAL EXPRESSION** ▶	Warm, Friendly Smiles, Making Eye Contact
Slouching, Hunching	◀ **BODY LANGUAGE** ▶	Good Posture, Standing Straight, and Confident
Outdated or Undone Hairstyle, Unfinished Make-up, Offensive, Non-Professional, Clothing (Stained or Wrinkled)	◀ **APPEARANCE** ▶	Updated, Fashion-Forward Hair Style, Fresh, Appropriate Make-Up, Fashionable Professional Clothing, Clean and Pressed
Unpleasant Smells, Body Odor, Smoke Smell, Bad Breath, Overpowering Perfume	◀ **PERSONAL HYGIENE** ▶	Pleasant Smells, Fresh Breath, Pleasing Aromas, Soft Fragrances

TIME FOR ACTION!

1. **What kind of impression does someone make when they don't smile or make eye contact?**

2. **Circle the Non-Verbal categories you'd like to work on:**

   Facial Expression • Body Language • Appearance • Personal Hygiene

3. **What kind of impact would those improvements have on your guests?**

KEY ELEMENTS OF

Top 20s are keenly aware and highly skilled in taking full advantage of those first few seconds in greeting new guests. A Top 20 Greeting is made of the following elements.

☐ **EYE CONTACT, SMILE, AND HELLO:** We begin easing the guest's tension by making eye contact, smiling, and saying hello. By greeting them this way, they will sense our interest and focus their attention on us. A smile says, "I am a nice person. It's safe to be with me."

☐ **SINCERE AND WARM WELCOME:** Welcoming the guest to the salon in a sincere way that warmly communicates, "I am happy to see you."

☐ **ACKNOWLEDGE GUEST'S NAME:** Most people love to hear the sound of their own name. Don't underestimate the Bonding power of using a guest's name correctly and often. Start questions and statements using their name.

☐ **INTRODUCE YOURSELF:** We confidently introduce ourselves to the guest by clearly stating our name.

☐ **SHAKING HANDS:** A socially acceptable and non-threatening way of making physical contact. A truly powerful piece of Non-Verbal Communication. So we extend our hand to the guest.

BONDING

☐ **GIVE DIRECTIONS:** Don't assume guests know what they are doing or where to go. The more informed guests are, the more comfortable they feel. Explaining where we are going, what to expect, and what we are going to do before we do it calms the guest.

☐ **GRACIOUSLY INVITE GUESTS BACK TO OUR STATION:**
So we escort—not race.

- *Walk next to them and make pleasant small talk.*

- *Keep attention and focus completely on them.*

- *Offer them a safe place to put their belongings.*

- *Turn the chair to face them and invite them to take a seat and make themselves comfortable.*

  - *A Genuine Compliment: find something to compliment them on.*

☐ **CREATE "YES MOMENTUM":** Getting our guests to say yes to purchase more services and products starts with creating "yes momentum" at the beginning of the appointment. Getting our guests to say "yes" to do little things like following us back to our station, sets the tone for getting bigger yeses later on. *"Let's go back to my station. Would that be ok?"* As our guests get into the "yes momentum," they become ready to say yes to important questions like:

"Would you like me to do that color service for you today?"

"Would you like to get started on the products we talked about today?"

BONDING BUSTERS

NERVOUS NELLY

Approaching guests in a timid, bashful, and shy manner that causes guests to be unsure of our skills.

RUMPLED, SHAGGY, AND SCRUFFY

Crawling out of bed and showing up for work looking disheveled, grubby, and ungroomed, sends messages to guests that we are messy and don't care.

FREQUENT FROWNER

Chronic non-smilers who always look like someone is holding a turd under their nose. Unaware that their scowling face sends threatening, unfriendly messages to their guests.

BAT OUTTA HELL

Racing out to greet a guest in a frenzied state. Blurting out their name followed by a "MEET ME AT THE BOWLS!" Then rushing off, leaving the guest dazed and confused.

The following are common examples of how we bust our opportunities to bond with guests when we fall into Bottom 80.

CRUDE RUDE MOOD

Vulgar, mean, gross, insulting, and obscene social manners that many guests and co-workers find offensive.

FUNKY SMELLS

Totally unaware of those body odors that trigger a gag response from guests: burps, too much perfume, BO, bad breath, gas or all the above!

ANNOYING TONES

High pitched, loud, shrill, piercing, agonizing, or irritating tones of voice that drive the guest crazy.

TIME FOR ACTION!

1. **Identify those Bonding Busters you can relate to most.**

2. **How do they bust your opportunities for Bonding?**

FOUR STEPS TO A

Top 20s know that Bonding with a new guest begins within the first ten seconds of the Greeting. Becoming highly skilled by practicing the following steps empowers us to quickly gain credibility and rapport with every guest we greet.

STEP 1 | INTRODUCTION

- Make eye contact and smile
- Say hello in a warm, sincere, and friendly voice

You can ease your guest's tension by simply looking into their eyes, smiling and saying "hello." Be in the moment and make it a point to consciously connect. They will sense your interest and will focus their attention on you. A smile says, "I am a nice person. It's safe to be with me."

STEP 2 | USE THEIR NAME

- Address guests by their name

People love the sound of their own name, so use it often. Practice starting questions and statements using their name.

STEP 3 | INTRODUCE YOURSELF TO NEW & REFERRAL GUESTS

- State your name clearly
- Shake the guest's hand
- Welcome the guest to the salon
- Offer a beverage

Find a greeting that works for you and then customize it by finding your own voice. Here is an example of how you might greet a new guest or a referral guest.

GREETING NEW OR REFERRAL GUEST: *"Hello Carmen, my name is Saige. Welcome. I'll be taking care of you today. It's nice to meet you. Can I get you something to drink?"*

GREETING

STEP 4

GIVING DIRECTIONS

- *Direct guests by telling them what to expect and where you will be taking them next*

- *Escort them to your station while making pleasant small talk—avoid rushing*

- *Let them know where to put their personal belongings*

- *Hold the styling chair for them as they sit*

- *Keep attention completely on the guest*

GIVING DIRECTIONS TO A NEW OR REFERRAL GUEST: *"Rachel, let's go back to my station, and we'll talk about what you'd like to do today. How does that sound? Here we are. Have a seat right here and make yourself comfortable. You can put your purse right over here."*

GIVING DIRECTIONS TO REPEAT GUEST:

"Amanda, let's go back to my station. There are some new looks I'd love to talk to you about."

101

BONDING SUMMARY

Bonding is the first step of the Power Wheel and it's all about **building credibility and rapport** with our guests. Bonding with guests is a major factor in achieving dramatic and sudden jumps in personal income. The positive impressions we make on our guests through Bonding gives them great feelings about the time and money they spend with us. This leads to much higher service and retail sales as well as greater repeat and referral business.

Feeling awkward and clumsy as we begin practicing new Bonding behaviors is perfectly normal, because we always feel that way whenever we're trying something for the first time. **But we must never confuse feelings of awkwardness with being phony or not being genuine with guests.**

Building a great clientele demands that we become highly skilled at Top 20 Bonding.

TOP 20 CREDIBILITY & RAPPORT OBSERVATION SHEET

Over the next few days, observe people around you both in and out of the salon and look for ways that they establish credibility and rapport.

⭐ Describe how the people you observed established credibility.

_____
_____
_____
_____
_____

⭐ How have you sabotaged your own credibility?

_____
_____
_____
_____
_____

⭐ What are 10 great credibility builders you observed?

_____
_____
_____
_____
_____

LIKE	TRUST	RESPECT
When the guest finds us enjoyable to be around.	When guests believe we have their best interest at heart.	When the guest believes we know what we're doing.

CREATE YOUR OWN TOP 20 GREETING

Using the FOUR STEPS TO A TOP 20 GREETING (pages 100–101), write your own scripts.

1: INTRODUCTION

- *Make eye contact and smile*
- *Say "hello" in a warm, sincere, and friendly voice*
- *Address guests by their name*

- *State your name clearly*
- *Shake hands*
- *Welcome guests to the salon*
- *Offer them a beverage*

Write your introduction for a new guest:

_____

_____

_____

Write your introduction for a repeat guest:

_____

_____

_____

2: GIVING DIRECTIONS

- *Direct guests by telling them what to expect and where we will be taking them next*

- *Let them know where to put their personal belongings*
- *Hold the styling chair for them as they sit*

Write your "giving directions" script for a new guest:

_____

_____

_____

Write your "giving directions" script for a repeat guest:

_____

_____

_____

COMMUNICATING SUCCESS

What kind of changes would I need to make to my Verbal, Non-Verbal, and Extra-Verbal communication styles if I wanted to make $_____ more per year? Use the Top 20 skills listed on pages 93–95 to help you fill in your answers.

VERBAL 5%: The words we use

EXTRA-VERBAL 35%: The feeling behind the words we use

NON-VERBAL 60%: The way we look and act

TOP 20 TS/BS GREETING EXERCISE

What is your greeting like when you're OVERWHELMED?

What kind of impression does that greeting make on the guest?

What are the possible results of an OVERWHELMED first impression?

What is your greeting like when you're ANNOYED?

What kind of impression does that greeting make on the guest?

What are the possible results of an ANNOYED first impression?

What is your greeting like when you're CONFIDENT?

What kind of impression does that greeting make on the guest?

What are the possible results of a CONFIDENT first impression?

Consulting

OVER THE TOP ⭐

Best Guest Practices of Top 20 Stylists

LESSON **6**

One of the most important factors that determines our financial success is our ability to give great consultations. When our guests don't buy more services and products, rebook their next appointment, or send us referrals, it's because they feel we didn't listen to them or we didn't understand or appreciate the look they wanted. Nothing closes the gap of misunderstanding of what our guest wants better than an extraordinary Consultation. This is why becoming highly skilled at Top 20 Consulting is so important.

KEY POINTS

- Technical Skills and Top 20 Consultations
- Creating Looks in Progress
- Raising Interest with the Right Purpose
- Opening Statements
- Asking Great Questions
- Listening to the Guest
- Paraphrasing
- Getting Permission and Offering Suggestions
- Asking for the Commitment
- Top 20 Responses to Guest Reactions

6 HAVE YOU EVER…

…been down this road?

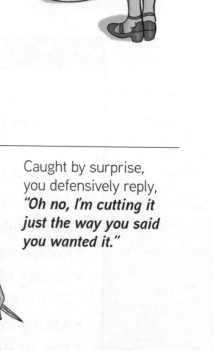

You ask your guest, *"So, how do you want your hair cut?"* The guest tells you what she wants, and you go to work on it.

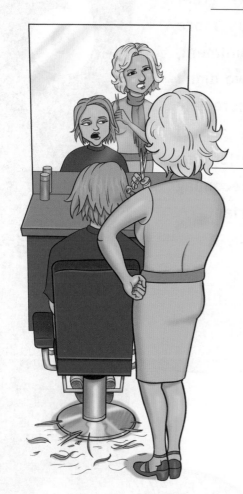

Halfway through the haircut, the guest shouts, *"You aren't cutting it too short up there, are you?"*

Caught by surprise, you defensively reply, *"Oh no, I'm cutting it just the way you said you wanted it."*

This kind of surprise tells us that there was a big gap between what the guest said and what we heard. This gap can be filled with a *Top 20 Consultation*.

1. CONSULTING

Consulting is the second step of the Power Wheel and it's about taking the time to have crucial conversations with our guests before the service begins. The purpose of Top 20 Consulting is to help guests find a fantastic look that they can get excited about. We do this by asking the right questions, discussing ideas, listening closely to the answers, offering the best services to achieve that look, and then agreeing on a plan of action.

2. BACK WHEEL SKILLS & TOP 20 CONSULTING

There is an important connection between our back wheel Technical Skills, and our success with Top 20 Consulting. The bicycle from Lesson 3 showed us that as we improve and expand our Technical Skills, we are able to offer a wider range of looks. We also learned that technical training can give us better language and greater self-confidence when describing these new looks to our guests. We must never underestimate the impact that our Technical Skills have on our ability to give Top 20 Consultations.

3. CREATING LOOKS IN PROGRESS

One of the biggest differences between Top 20 **BLUE** and Bottom 80 **RED** is that stylists stuck in Bottom 80 "**do hair**." Their consultations are all about the type of haircut the guest wants done today. Top 20s **create "looks in progress."** *What are looks in progress?* They are looks that evolve over several visits. Top 20 stylists focus their consultation on coming into an agreement with guests about the look they want, and the services needed to begin evolving that look. Top 20s are highly skilled in choosing the best services, tools, and products for creating fantastic looks.

WHAT MAKES UP AN EVOLVING LOOK?

- Haircut
- Color
- Texture
- Conditioning Treatments
- Chemical Services
- Additional Services
- Finishing Tools
- Retail Products
  - Home Haircare
  - Styling Products

Every time we come into an agreement with our guests about an evolving look, we are creating a need for them to receive more services, rebook a repeat visit, and take home retail products.

Moving from "doing hair" to "creating looks" demands that we develop the eyes to see beyond the haircut. When looking at fashion pictures try to identify the type of services, products, and tools that were used to create that look.

4. STYLE PORTFOLIO/LOOK BOOK

A Style Portfolio or Look Book contains pictures of styles and the services needed to create them. Creating our own Look Book gives us the confidence to show and discuss these looks with our guests because we know we can achieve them. It also helps us close the gap between what a guest is saying and what we are hearing. This understanding opens the door for discussions about new services we feel confident doing. **When we shift the conversation from getting a haircut to creating a look in progress, we will never have to sell again because guests automatically become interested in the services and products we are offering.**

Many times guests bring pictures with them to describe what they want. Stylists stuck in Bottom 80 have a tendency to get annoyed at guests who do this. They think things like: "I am so sick of seeing that movie star's hair. There is no way she can have that look. Does she think I can work miracles?"

Oftentimes behind that kind of a BS attitude is a fear of failure. "What if I can't make it look like the picture?" or "I don't know how to do this."

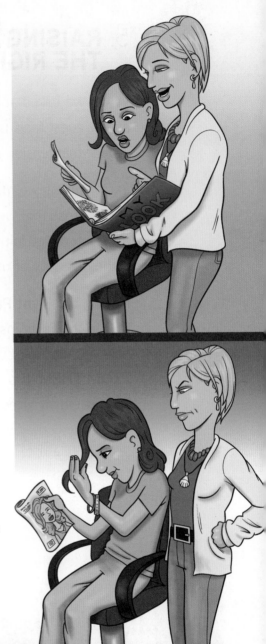

TIME FOR ACTION!

1. **What are some Technical Skills you have learned that would make a difference in how you talk to a guest during the Consultation?**

2. **What are some ideas for putting a Style Portfolio/Look Book together?**

5. **RAISING INTEREST WITH THE RIGHT PURPOSE**

When we talked about Bonding in the last chapter, we discussed the tension a new guest feels upon meeting us for the first time. We saw how we could reduce that tension quickly by greeting guests warmly and putting them at ease.

In Consulting we must raise another kind of energy—**interest.** When a guest gets a sense that we are interested in them and what they want, they become more interested in us, and what we want FOR them. Having the Right Purpose is the best way of truly showing our guests that we are interested in them.

Having the Right Purpose is about being more interested in what we want FOR our guests instead of what we want FROM our guests. Many stylists believe that their purpose is to get their guests to buy services and products **FROM THEM**. If selling is our purpose, our guests will feel sold, and we will feel like pushy sales people.

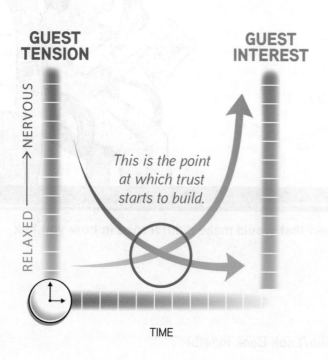

GUEST TENSION

GUEST INTEREST

NERVOUS

RELAXED

This is the point at which trust starts to build.

TIME

But when our guests get a sense that our purpose **FOR THEM** is to give them a look that they feel great about and a look that they can recreate at home, they become a lot more interested. In fact there is a critical point during the Consultation when tension falls and interest rises. When these two points intersect, we have achieved trust. When guests trust us, they listen better and are more likely to take us up on service suggestions we make.

6. **THE OPENING STATEMENT**

Telling our guests what we want **FOR** them is a great way to begin a Top 20 Consultation. This is called an **Opening Statement**. The following examples communicate the right purpose, raise guest interest, and include a permission request, which allows us to move forward with discovery questions.

NEW GUEST OPENING STATEMENT: *"It's important to me that you have a look that you feel great about, and a look that you're going to be able to do at home. So, before I get started, I'd like to ask you a few questions. Would that be alright?"*

REPEAT GUEST OPENING STATEMENT: *"It's been a few visits since I checked in with you about what we've been doing with your hair. I always want to make sure that your look is fresh and up-to-date. So I'm thinking, we could take a couple minutes to talk. How does that sound?"*

On the other hand, if our goal is to get something FROM our guests, our opening statement would sound something like this. "It's important to me that you spend as much of your money with me as possible, so I will be pushing you really hard to get more services and make sure you buy a bunch of my retail and for sure rebook your next appointment. How does that sound?"

Now we would never say anything like that, but when our purpose is to get something FROM our guests, it creates an energy that they pick up on. They then lose interest in us and what we have to offer. But the correct use of an Opening Statement sets the stage for us to ask a variety of questions and gives us the opening to make service suggestions later on.

My goal today is to get as much of your money as possible!

TIME FOR ACTION!

1. List what we traditionally want FROM our guests.

2. List what we traditionally want FOR our guests.

3. Using your FOR list, write an Opening Statement for:

   A NEW GUEST:

   A REPEAT GUEST:

4. What could happen if our Opening Statement has the wrong intention?

7. DISCOVERING PROBLEMS WITH QUESTIONS

Another important part of Top 20 Consulting is to solve our guest's haircare problems. Haircare problems are the difference between what guests HAVE that they don't WANT, or, what guests WANT and don't HAVE. Most guests need help identifying and describing the problems they are having with their look. Our job is to help them by asking the right questions to get them talking about their problems and then offering the services they need to solve their problems, and get what they want.

Therefore we need to find out what they like and don't like, what they have and don't want, and what they want and don't have. Asking our guests the right questions enables them to give us the information we need. **This information is extremely valuable because it helps us to determine the services needed to create the looks our guests desire.** The right open-ended or multiple choice questions will get our guests talking about their haircare problems.

OPEN-ENDED QUESTIONS: Open-Ended questions are questions that require **more than a "yes" or "no" answer.** They generally start with what, why, and how. EXAMPLE: *"What types of challenges are you having when you style your hair?"*

MULTIPLE CHOICE QUESTIONS: Multiple Choice questions are especially useful in helping guests who are unable to describe their haircare problems or are unsure of what they want. These types of questions provide descriptive choices that make it easier for our guests to answer. Creating a multiple choice list of descriptive **"want"** and **"have"** words helps our guests to easily identify what they want.

EXAMPLE: *"What are some qualities you would like to see more of in the color of your hair? More warmth? More richness?"*

8. **HAVE, WANT, & CAUSE QUESTIONS**

There are three types of Open-Ended and Multiple Choice questions: HAVE, WANT, and CAUSE. **Using the right questions DIRECTS our guests, which helps them find the right service and product solutions.**

HAVE QUESTIONS:
What do you have that you don't want?

These types of questions help to identify what guests have that they don't want. Typical Open-Ended, Multiple Choice HAVE questions might be: *"What kinds of problems do you have when you style your hair at home? Is it hard to manage, time-consuming, not turning out how you'd like it to?"*

WANT QUESTIONS:
What do you want that you don't have?

When asking what guests "want," their choices become more important because often guests aren't aware of what the possibilities are. This type of question could help narrow it down. An Open-Ended, Multiple Choice WANT question may sound like this: *"What qualities would you like to see more of in your hairstyle? Fullness? Shine? Depth? Richness?"*

CAUSE QUESTIONS:
What do you think is causing the problem?

With CAUSE questions we are looking for what might be causing problems with our guest's hair. For example we know that heat from dryers, flat irons, or curling irons play a role in damaging hair as well as sun, chlorine, or other environmental conditions. An example of a CAUSE question could be: *"What kinds of styling tools are you using at home?"*

TOP 20 QUESTION TOOLBOX

OPEN-ENDED QUESTIONS: Get our guests talking about their look.

What do you like most about your hair now?

What is your favorite hairstyle?

What great styles have you seen lately?

What are your concerns when thinking about coloring your hair?

What is it about this picture that you like?

HAVE QUESTIONS: What guests have that they don't want.

What would you consider a bad hair day?

What do you dislike about your current look?

What challenges are you having with your hair?

CAUSE QUESTIONS: Pinpoints what might be causing the problem.

What do you think would make your hairstyle easier?

How are you feeling about the current condition of your hair?

MULTIPLE CHOICE QUESTIONS:

Provides descriptive choices that are easier for our guests to answer.

What are some qualities you would like to see more of in the color of your hair? More warmth? More richness?

What challenges are you having with your hair? Does it feel weak? Has it lost its shine?

WANT QUESTIONS: Makes guests aware of what the possibilities are.

If your haircolor could look anyway you wanted it to look, how would it look?

If your hair were exactly the way you wanted it to be what would that look like?

If you could have any celebrity's hair, who would that be?

What are you looking for in a haircolor service?

COLOR CONVERSATION STARTERS:

Not all of our guests receive color services from us. Here are some great ways to get the color conversation started.

"I was looking forward to seeing you today! I just attended an amazing class that introduced the latest breakthrough in haircolor, and I would love to tell you about it. Would that be OK?"

"I've been thinking about how we could enhance your look in a subtle way. I would like you to look at some pictures. Your hair is similar to this style, but the difference is the dimension around the front. We could place a few foils here and here and achieve a beautiful subtle change with just a little bit of color. How does that sound?"

TIME FOR ACTION!

1. What are some of the problems guests share with you about their current look?

2. What are some of the words guests use to describe what they:

   WANT that they don't have?

   HAVE that they don't want?

3. What are two questions from pages 115–117 that would help you better understand the kind of look your guest is interested in? Rewrite those questions using your own words.

   a.

   b.

4. Using the COLOR CONVERSATION STARTERS on page 117, write a script for getting a color conversation started with guests who are not currently color guests.

9. LISTENING TO THE GUEST

Asking our guests the right questions is an important skill to have, but it will get us nowhere if we lack the skill to listen and hear their answers. When we were young we learned to speak, we learned to write, we learned to read. But how many of us ever took a listening course? And yet, effective listening is one of the most important tools Top 20s call on every day with every guest.

The main reason our guests don't buy more services and products, rebook, or send us referrals, is because they feel we didn't listen, understand, or appreciate the look they wanted. **Nothing closes the gap of misunderstanding of what our guests want better than Top 20 Listening Skills.**

The most effective way to listen is with an open, calm, and quiet mind. Developing Top 20 Listening Skills means making use of all the Verbal, Extra-Verbal, and Non-Verbal Communication between us and our guests. Top 20 Listening helps us quickly and effectively close the gap between what guests tell us they want and our understanding of what they are saying. There are three parts that make up Top 20 Listening Skills: **Guest-Centered Listening**, **Non-Judgmental Listening**, and **Focused Listening**.

Listening is defined as, "hearing with the intent to understand." It sounds simple enough. *So what keeps us from accomplishing this task?* Bottom 80 Listening Habits.

The following are three of the many self-limiting Bottom 80 Listening Habits. **Self-Centered Listening**, **Judgmental Listening**, and **Distracted Listening**. Bottom 80 Listening Habits cause misunderstanding and lead to guest loss.

10. **GUEST-CENTERED LISTENING**

Guest-Centered Listening is about giving our full attention to the guest and what the guest is sharing with us with nothing else on our mind. When we listen this way we are able to ask great questions and get answers that help us better serve our guests. When we use this kind of listening, we send this message to our guests: "You are important and I'm interested in what you have to say." When guests sense this attitude, they are more likely to open up and trust our recommendations.

An extraordinary guest experience is the end result of centering our full attention on our guests.

11. **SELF-CENTERED LISTENING**

Self-Centered Listening is when we have ourselves and our lives on our minds when we are supposed to be listening to our guest. Self-Centered Listening isn't bad, but it is a common habit that keeps us stuck in Bottom 80. The things we are thinking about may be positive or negative: things like family, bills, a new car, a date, or a relationship problem. Of course these things need our attention and may even be more interesting than what the guest is saying, but we end up not being able to focus on our guest's needs and wants. When we are in Self-Centered Listening, we are really only listening to ourselves. Becoming skillful at Top 20 Consultations will be extremely difficult until we break the habit of Self-Centered listening.

120

12. **NON-JUDGMENTAL LISTENING**

Being Non-Judgmental empowers us with the confidence and wisdom to understand what our guests are trying to tell us.

Instead of judging what guests are telling us or deciding if we like them or not, we are more interested in listening to what they want. We avoid jumping to conclusions or interrupting them by finishing their sentences. Sometimes we may still not think that what they want will work for them, but by listening this way we are able to hear them out and then make suggestions that are not filled with judgment and sarcasm. **Non-Judgmental Listening opens us up for gaining greater understanding of our guests and what they are trying to tell us.** Listening this way gives our guests the feeling of being understood and makes them more receptive to the ideas and suggestions we offer them.

13. **JUDGMENTAL LISTENING**

Judgmental Listening is when we are judging or criticizing **ourselves** or our **guests**. Our mind is busy judging or pre-judging our guests, what they're saying, how they look, or what they want. In our head it may sound like this, *"I can't stand this guest," "That is the stupidest thing I have ever heard," "Does she think I'm a magician,"* or *"What's this guest think of me?"* or *"Oh no, I don't think I can do what she wants me to do."* Judgmental Listening leads to misunderstanding and a dissatisfied guest who isn't interested in the services and retail we have to offer or in coming back as a repeat guest.

JUDGMENTAL LISTENING ALSO INCLUDES:
- *Jumping to conclusions*
- *Over-reacting*
- *Interrupting or finishing sentences*
- *Agreeing or disagreeing*
- *Evaluating others or even ourselves*

121

14. FOCUSED LISTENING

Focused Listening is about giving our full attention to the guest and not allowing ourselves to be distracted by what's going on around us. Guests are always sending cues and clues to us throughout the entire consulting process. It only takes a second for us to miss something critical that could make all the difference for the rest of the appointment. If we are using Focused Listening, we'll catch many of these messages. They usually appear in the form of "wants" or "wishes." Sometimes they'll show up as "don't wants" or "get rid ofs." Focused Listening helps us to determine what services to offer our guests that address the problems or concerns they bring up.

Not allowing day-to-day distractions to take our focus off our guests enables us to hear and respond to important guest messages.

15. DISTRACTED LISTENING

The third listening habit of stylists stuck in Bottom 80 is called Distracted Listening. It's when our attention is on other things that are going on in the salon. Life in the salon is filled with distractions. In fact **the average person is distracted 22 minutes out of every hour.** Where else can we hear six conversations going on at the same time? People walking by, music in the background, blow dryers roaring, looking at ourself in the mirror. It's no wonder that Distracted Listening is so dangerous. Because when guests sense we are distracted, they get the feeling that we don't really care about them and they are less likely to be interested in all of the great ideas we have for them. Also, when we are distracted, we tend to be forgetful and as a result we may forget the answers guests give us that can lead to more service and product sales.

16. *STOP!* NOT NOW

All of us have the potential to be Top 20 Listeners and the best way to achieve that is by avoiding Self-Centered, Judgmental, or Distracted listening habits. The first step to become a Top 20 Listener is by practicing NCT: Name, Claim, and Tame. Naming and Claiming our Bottom 80 Listening habits allows us to break out of them by using the Taming action of "Stop! Not Now."

Every time we see ourselves slipping into Self-Centered, Judgmental, or Distracted Listening, simply say, **"Stop! Not Now."** From there we redirect our attention back to our guest. For some of us who are used to listening from Bottom 80, we may need to catch ourselves frequently. But it is well worth the effort because it can instantly bring us to Top 20 Listening.

Anytime you slip into Bottom 80 Listening, silently say to yourself, "Stop! Not Now." and then redirect your attention back to the guest.

80/20 LISTENING COMPARISON

▶ **SELF-CENTERED LISTENING**
- Preoccupied with ourselves.
- Listening to ourselves, not the guests.

▶ **GUEST-CENTERED LISTENING**
- Our mind is on the guests, not self.
- Giving our guests our undivided attention.

▶ **JUDGMENTAL LISTENING**
- Judging our guests and what they are saying.
- Judging ourselves and our abilities.
- Jumping to conclusions.

▶ **NON-JUDGMENTAL LISTENING**
- No opinions or judgments of our guests.
- No negative judgments about ourselves.
- Listening with an open mind.

▶ **DISTRACTED LISTENING**
- Being easily distracted by what's going on around us.
- Inability to stay focused.

▶ **FOCUSED LISTENING**
- Giving full attention to our guests.
- Not allowing distractions to take our attention off our guests.

TIME FOR ACTION!

1. **Give an example of each of the Bottom 80 Listening habits.**

   a. *Self-Centered*

   b. *Judgmental*

   c. *Distracted*

2. **How does it make you feel when you can tell someone is listening to you from...**

   a. *Self-Centered?*

   b. *Judgmental?*

   c. *Distracted?*

3. **How could you practice using the Taming action of "STOP! NOT NOW." with...**

   a. *Guests?*

   b. *Co-workers?*

   c. *Friends?*

17. PARAPHRASING

Guests don't return to us when they feel like we didn't give them what they asked for. There was a gap between what they were trying to tell us they wanted and what we gave them. All arguments or misunderstandings between our guests and ourselves can be traced back to not closing this gap.

Paraphrasing is a great gap-closing technique that can prevent misunderstanding and guest loss. **Paraphrasing is about restating back to the guest in our own words what we hear them saying. It's the proof that we've been listening.** Our first few efforts at paraphrasing may sound forced or phony. However, as we get skillful, it will become a natural part of our consulting process.

PARAPHRASING EXAMPLE:

"Let me see if I understand what you're looking for. It sounds like you would like a look that gives your hair more body, more depth, and more richness in the color and is easier to take care of. <u>Do I have this right?</u>"

TOP 20 CONSULTATION STEP 5

18. GETTING PERMISSION AND OFFERING SUGGESTIONS

Through the process of asking Open-Ended questions and practicing Top 20 Listening, we discover critical information about our guest's hair. It's important to be able to utilize this information as we suggest the services and products that best fit the look our guest wants.

Our intention in this phase of Consulting is to help guests find out what they need to **DO, USE, and BUY** in order to get what they want. For many guests this means multiple service solutions such as haircuts, glazes, foils, lightening, darkening, corrective color, conditioning treatments, texture services, or any combination of the above.

GETTING PERMISSION AND OFFERING SUGGESTIONS EXAMPLE:

We begin this part of the consultation by getting our guests' permission to offer suggestions. **Getting the guests' permission gives them the feeling of being involved and in control.**

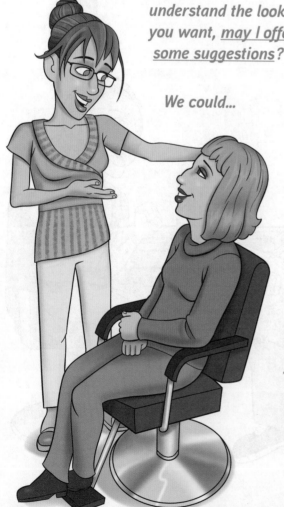

"Now that I understand the look you want, may I offer some suggestions?

We could...

...Add movement, take out weight, and incorporate some layers...

...Add warmth with color, add depth with lowlights...

HOW TO OFFER SUGGESTIONS

THAT RELATE TO THE HAIRCUT: *"You mentioned that you don't care for your hair when it's cut too short. What if we keep length by trimming it slightly and creating more movement at the bottom with longer layers? And when I style your hair, I'll teach you some easy tips for different looks. That way you can wear it smooth, straight, or kick it up with a little curl. How's that sound?"*

FOR HAIR COLOR SERVICES: *"As we were talking you mentioned that the color of your hair was OK, but you weren't crazy about it. With a little bit of color we could jazz it up with subtle dimension that would look naturally shiny and beautiful. I'm suggesting we do some soft highlights around the front and some lowlights throughout the sides and back. How does that sound?"*

FOR CONDITIONING TREATMENTS: *"After looking at your hair and considering what you've shared with me, may I suggest that we formulate a customized chemistry treatment for you today? This treatment is long lasting, up to 21 days, and gives your hair the qualities you're looking for. How does that sound?"*

FOR A WAXING SERVICE: *"Most of my guests have me take care of their eyebrows. We could really get a nice shape to them. I would be more than happy to do that for you. How does that sound?"*

...Focus on your eyes with a brow wax...

...Add more strength, shine and body with a custom chemistry."

Now we can combine the information we received from the guest with the SERVICES we're suggesting.

This gracefully moves us to the next step of the process, which is asking the guest to BUY.

19. ASKING GUESTS TO BUY SERVICES

STEP 6

The easiest and safest way to ask guests if they would like to try the services we're suggesting is by using the S.A.N.S. approach; Smile–Ask–Nod–Shut Up.

S **SMILE AS YOU ASK THE QUESTION.**

A **ASK THE QUESTION.** *"I have time. Would you like me to do that for you today?" or "This custom treatment is only $__. Would you like me to do that for you today?"*

N **NOD YOUR HEAD GENTLY AS YOU ASK THE QUESTION.**

S **SHUT UP.** Don't say anything more. Let the guest talk.

BOTTOM 80 ASKING BLUNDERS

"Would you like me to color your hair today?...	*...or no?"*
"Would you like me to do that for you today?...	*...or did you want to wait until next time?"*
"Did you want me to do those highlights today?...	*...or do you want to think about it?"*

TIME FOR ACTION!

1. What did you learn about Paraphrasing, Getting Permission, and Offering Suggestions that you didn't know before?

2. What is your biggest fear about asking your guests to buy a service?

3. Give an example of how a Bottom 80 Asking Blunder sabotaged your ability to sell more services.

20. TOP 20 RESPONSES TO GUEST REACTIONS

Once we've asked the guest if they would like to purchase the service we've offered, there are a handful of guest reactions that we should anticipate getting. The better we are at gauging and understanding our guests' reactions, the more prepared we are to give a Top 20 response.

GUEST: *"Do you have time to do this for me today?"*

These are guests who want to go for all of our suggested services. We call these guests "gifts." They make our job easy.

> **TOP 20 RESPONSE:** *"I'd love to do that for you today."*

GUEST: *"No, I need to think about it"* **or** *"No, not today.* **or** *"No, I don't have extra money for that."*

When our guests say "no," the most important thing we can do is to not take it personally and stop feeling like a dork. We must realize that every time we make any offerings, we're planting seeds of opportunity to evolve their look over future visits.

> **TOP 20 RESPONSE:** *"I understand. Let me jot down what we talked about today so that if you decide to do this later on, I have a record of what we discussed."*

GUEST: *"How much does it cost?"*

This question is usually an indicator that our guests are interested in the service we're offering them, but need clarity about the cost before moving forward. The most important thing we can do in this situation is to not panic. Instead simply answer their question with confidence and allow them to choose.

> **TOP 20 RESPONSE:** *"The charge for that service would be $_____ and would take about _____ minutes. Would you like me to do that for you today?"*

The good news is, the more skillful we get at service offerings, the more yeses we'll get from our guests.

KEY ELEMENTS OF

Top 20s know how important a consultation is to helping guests find fantastic looks they can get excited about. The following elements of a Top 20 Consultation make that possible.

☐ **STYLE PORTFOLIO/LOOK BOOK:** Create a binder (or a phone or tablet gallery!) that contains pictures of looks that were created with a variety of services. Using pictures helps us recommend an entire look rather than just a haircut. Find pictures of looks that we feel confident offering.

☐ **FACE-TO-FACE AND HANDS OFF:** We should face guests at eye level, and avoid talking to them in the mirror during the beginning of the consultation. This helps us make a direct connection with guests, and it also makes it harder for us to put our hands in their hair. We want to avoid putting our hands in their hair so there is plenty of room for the guests to put their own hands up there. Often guests will be able to express themselves more clearly if they can show us what they want or the problems they have, by using their own hair as a visual aid. That way when we ask a question like, *"What kinds of problems do you have when you try to style your hair at home?"* they can use their hands in their own hair to show us.

☐ **BEGIN WITH AN OPENING STATEMENT:** An Opening Statement at the beginning of the consultation can set the tone for the rest of the appointment. A good Opening Statement makes two promises: first, it helps our guests find a look they are going to love, and second, it makes sure they can take care of their look at home. *"It's important to me that you have a look that you feel great about, and a look that you're going to be able to do at home. So, before I get started, I'd like to ask you a few questions. Would that be OK?"*

☐ **ASK OPEN-ENDED QUESTIONS:** Great questions get our guests talking about what they like and don't like, more importantly what they want or don't want. *"What types of challenges are you having with your hair when you style it at home? Is it difficult to manage? Do you have trouble getting it to stay?"*

CONSULTING

☐ **LISTEN:** Practice *"Stop! Not Now."* whenever we catch ourselves slipping into Self-Centered, Judgmental, or Distracted Listening and get right back to Top 20 Listening.

☐ **USE A CLIPBOARD:** This shows our guests that we care enough to record and monitor what we talk about. When we use a clipboard, we appear to be organized, prepared, and efficient. It is also a great place to hide notes, questions, and scripts.

☐ **PARAPHRASE:** Repeating back to the guest what we heard is a great gap-closing technique that can prevent misunderstanding and guest loss. *"It sounds like you would like a look that gives your hair more body, more depth, more richness in the color, and is easier to take care of. <u>Do I have this right?</u>"*

☐ **GETTING PERMISSION & OFFERING SUGGESTIONS:** Getting our guests' permission to offer a suggestion or a service before we actually present it is a great way to keep our guests involved. *"Now that we understand the look you want, may I offer some suggestions to achieve and maintain your look?"*

☐ **ASKING WITH S.A.N.S.:** Use the SANS approach to ask guests if they would like to try the services we're suggesting. Remember to avoid the Asking Blunders (page 128).

S **<u>Smile</u>** as you ask the question

A **<u>Ask</u>** the question,
"I have time. Would you like me to do that for you today?"

N **<u>Nod</u>** your head gently as you ask the question.

S **<u>Shut up.</u>** Don't say anything more. Let the guest talk.

CONSULTATION CRUSHERS

SPEED DEMON

Speeding through the consultation and assuming we know what they want. We're often interrupting guests by saying: "Yeah-yeah-yeah, I got it! Let's go ahead and get going."

THE NOTs

Not paying attention.
Not asking questions.
Not taking notes.
Not making offerings.
Not going to succeed!

FRAIDY-CAT

Never offering services because we're afraid guests will say no, we're running behind, or we're worried about the service blowing up on us! In fact, we're afraid of just about everything.

SAME OLD, SAME OLD, ONE-CUT WONDERS

Because it's been such a long time since attending any kind of advanced training, we've fallen into the rut of complacency. Doing the same old look on the same old guest in the same old way... year... after year... after year... after year.

YEAR 1

YEAR 3

YEAR 5

The following are common examples of how we crush opportunities for greater income when we fall into Bottom 80 Consulting.

PICTURE HATRED

Hating it when guests bring in pictures or point to any kind of picture book because their look never turns out like the picture. Guests have unrealistic expectations and, "If I have to cut that starlet's look one more time I'm going to barf!"

HANDS IN THE HAIR

As soon as the guest sits in our chair we immediately put our hands into their hair and start playing with it, leaving no room for our guests to show us what they want.

MIRROR TALKER

Instead of making eye contact with the guest, they talk to themselves in the mirror. Mirror talking is great for those who can't get enough of admiring their own image.

TIME FOR ACTION!

1. **Identify those Consultation Crushers you can relate to the most.**

2. **How does the one you chose crush opportunities to sell more services in your consultation?**

SIX STEPS TO A

Top 20s become highly skilled by practicing the following steps. These steps empower us to quickly discover a great look for our guests and help us to offer services to create that look.

STEP 1	**BEGIN WITH AN OPENING STATEMENT**

Using an opening statement sets the stage for us to ask a variety of questions and enables us to make service suggestions later on.

NEW GUEST OPENING STATEMENT: *"When I begin working with someone new, I like to take the time to ask a few questions. It's important to me that you have a look that you feel great about, and a look that you're going to be able to do at home. Would that be OK?"*

REPEAT GUEST OPENING STATEMENT: *"You know what? It's been a few visits since I checked in with you about what we've been doing with your hair. I always want to make sure that your look is fresh and up-to-date. So I'm thinking we could take a couple minutes to talk. Would that be OK?"*

STEP 2	**ASK OPEN–ENDED QUESTIONS**

Great questions get our guests talking about what they like, and don't like, and more importantly, what they want and don't want.

OPEN-ENDED EXAMPLE: *"If you could have your hair any way you wanted it, how would it look?"* or *"What challenges are you experiencing with your hair?"*

STEP 3	**LISTEN AND WRITE DOWN ANSWERS ON YOUR CLIPBOARD**

Top 20 Listening helps us to quickly and effectively close the gap between what the guest is telling us they want and our understanding of what they are saying. Recording some notes about guests' likes, dislikes, and possible services comes in handy for future visits.

CONSULTATION

STEP 4 PARAPHRASE

Once we have asked questions and listened to our guests' answers, a great way to make sure there is no gap between what they are saying and what we are hearing is to paraphrase in our own words.

PARAPHRASE EXAMPLE: *"I want to make sure I understand what you're looking for. It sounds like you would like a look that is just a bit shorter, and then doing something with the color to brighten up the look. <u>Does that sound right?</u>"*

STEP 5 GETTING PERMISSION & OFFERING SUGGESTIONS

Getting our guests' permission to offer suggestions or services before we actually present it arouses their curiosity and piques their interest in the great possibilities for their look. *"Now that we understand the look you want, may I offer some suggestions to achieve and maintain your look?"*

SERVICE SUGGESTION: *"Color plays a big role in the look we're moving toward. We can really do something interesting with some soft highlights around the front and some lowlights throughout the sides and back. This is what it would look like. <u>How does that sound?</u>"*

STEP 6 ASK FOR THE COMMITMENT

Use the S.A.N.S. approach.

S: Smile.

A: Ask the question. *"I have time to do that color for you today. Would you like me to do that for you?"*

N: Nod.

S: Shut up.

CONSULTING SUMMARY

One of the main reasons new guests don't buy more services and products, rebook, or come back as repeat guests, is because they feel we didn't listen, didn't understand, or didn't appreciate the look they wanted. When we fail to check in and re-consult with our repeat guests, they begin to feel taken for granted and end up going somewhere else in order to get a fresh perspective and a new look.

Each and every Top 20 Consultation we do contains enormous potential for greater financial growth. This potential is hidden from us whenever we're stuck in Bottom 80. **Becoming highly skilled at doing Top 20 Consultations is crucial to building a great clientele.**

ANATOMY OF A LOOK

Tape a fashion hairstyle here and make a list of all of the services and products needed to create that look.

LIST OF SERVICES

CREATING A STYLE PORTFOLIO/LOOK BOOK

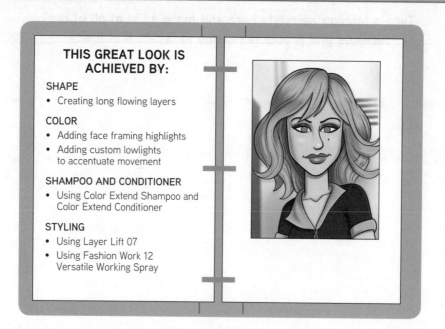

THIS GREAT LOOK IS ACHIEVED BY:

SHAPE
• Creating long flowing layers

COLOR
• Adding face framing highlights
• Adding custom lowlights to accentuate movement

SHAMPOO AND CONDITIONER
• Using Color Extend Shampoo and Color Extend Conditioner

STYLING
• Using Layer Lift 07
• Using Fashion Work 12 Versatile Working Spray

Make your Look Book more interesting by including the details of HOW the look is achieved. Study the look and answer the following questions.

a. *What type of haircut is needed?*

b. *What type of color services were used to achieve this look?*

c. *What texturizing services were used?*

d. *What home haircare products are needed to maintain this healthy look?*

e. *What styling products and tools were used?*

f. *What additional services were used to achieve this overall look? Eyebrows? Make-up?*

g. *Do I feel confident in my skills to achieve this look?*

TOP 20 SERVICE OFFERING WORKSHEET

1. What is a color service that you wish more of your guests bought from you?

2. In the **BACK WHEEL** write a Technical Description of a service.

3. Now translate that into language your guests would understand using descriptive words in the **FRONT WHEEL**.

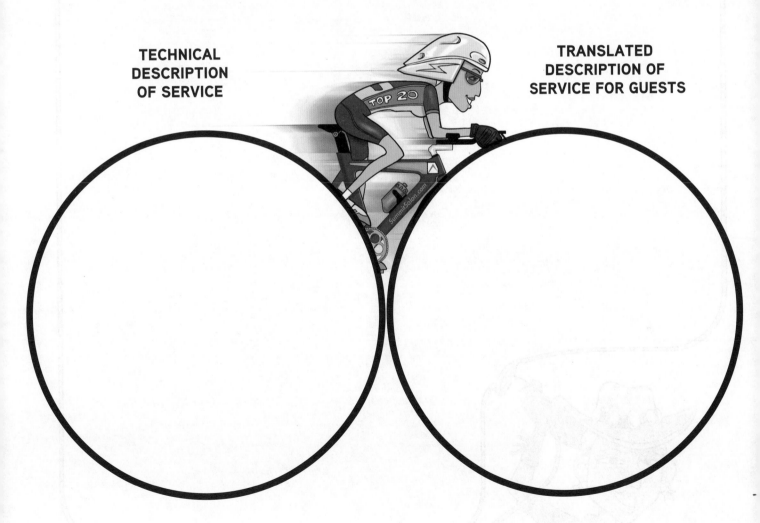

TECHNICAL DESCRIPTION OF SERVICE

TRANSLATED DESCRIPTION OF SERVICE FOR GUESTS

TOP 20 QUESTIONS WORKSHEET

GREAT QUESTION ROUND UP!

Use this sheet to start rounding up great questions that get your guests talking about their look. Start testing these questions with guests and co-workers. Highlight the ones that seem to get the best response.

© Summit Salon Business Center, LLC *SummitSalon.com*

TOP 20 CONSULTATION SCRIPT WORKSHEET

Create your own Top 20 Consultation by writing your own scripts for
Steps 1, 2, 5, and 6. Get a clipboard and begin using it with your guests.

1: WRITE OPENING STATEMENTS

New Guest Opening Statement:

_____

_____

Repeat Guest Opening Statement:

_____

_____

2: WRITE OPEN-ENDED QUESTIONS

_____

_____

_____

_____

3: Listen and write down answers on your clipboard. Practice *"Stop! Not Now."*

4: Paraphrase back to the guest what you heard.

5: GET PERMISSION AND OFFER SUGGESTIONS

_____

_____

_____

6: ASK FOR THE COMMITMENT (S.A.N.S.)

_____

_____

_____

_____

TOP 20 CONSULTATION DISCOVERY SHEET

Use this sheet during a consultation to practice becoming aware of all the things to learn about your guest. What we learn here will be very helpful during the Servicing and Finishing Steps.

GUEST'S NAME: _____

WHAT HAIR PROBLEMS DO THEY HAVE THAT THEY DON'T WANT?

_____

_____

WHAT QUALITIES DO THEY WANT THAT THEY DON'T HAVE?

_____

_____

POSSIBLE SERVICE SUGGESTIONS:

_____

_____

POSSIBLE HOME HAIRCARE PRODUCTS:

_____

_____

STYLING SUGGESTIONS AND POSSIBLE STYLING PRODUCTS:

_____

_____

REBOOK CLUES (SEE *LISTENING FOR GUEST MESSAGES* ON PAGE 186):

_____

_____

POSSIBLE REFERRALS TO ASK ABOUT:

_____

_____

Servicing

The Servicing process is the longest part of a guest's appointment and provides us with many opportunities to use our Technical and Communication Skills in ways that make our guests look and feel great. Guests return to us, send in referrals, and buy more of our services and products because the experience they have in our chair is extraordinary. This is called *Top 20 Service*. Developing Top 20 Service Skills is a major key to achieving sudden and dramatic jumps in personal income.

KEY POINTS

- Three Essential Parts of Top 20 Servicing
- Technical Skills and Servicing
- Balancing the Conversation
- Managing the Relationship
- Selling Home Haircare
- Rebooking Guests

7 HAVE YOU EVER NOTICED...

...how nervous guests get whenever they have been sitting alone with haircolor on their head?

Anytime they see someone walk by they say things like: *"Can you find my hairdresser? I think she forgot about me and I know I'm done."*

And then someone runs into the back room and yells, *"Hey, you better get out there right now because you've got a color guest going psycho!"*

This of course catches us off guard, embarrasses us, and makes us annoyed.

On the way over to them we say to ourselves, *"How rude! They must think I'm stupid! I know what I'm doing! She's not even done yet! I've got five more minutes before I have to take it off for crying out loud!"*

This is a common example of what happens to guests who are left uninformed, uninvolved, and all alone with chemical on their head.

Top 20 Servicing is all about preventing these kinds of events from happening.

1. SERVICING

Servicing is the third step of the Power Wheel and is best defined as providing our guests with an extraordinary service experience. This is called Top 20 Service. The single biggest reason our guests return to us, send in referrals, and buy more of our services and products is because the experience they have in our chair is extraordinary. When we give Top 20 Service, our guests' level of anxiety is low and their interest is high, and as a result, they feel good about themselves, are willing to spend more money, and build a trusting relationship with us.

THERE ARE THREE ESSENTIAL PARTS THAT MAKE UP *Top 20 Servicing:*

PART 1:   *Balancing guest conversations and managing guest relationships.*

PART 2:   *Selling home haircare products.*

PART 3:   *Getting guests to rebook their next appointment.*

Becoming keenly aware and highly skilled at the three essential parts of Top 20 Servicing is critical to achieving sudden jumps in personal income.

2. TECHNICAL SKILLS AND TOP 20 SERVICE

There is a direct connection between our Technical Skills and our ability to give Top 20 Service. Strong Technical Skills automatically empower us with the ability to offer our guests a wider range of new looks. Understanding the products used to produce outstanding technical results is an absolute must. The skillful use of the right product can make a huge difference. This is why it's so important to build the Technical Skills of the back wheel of our bicycle.

As our skills go up so does our self-confidence.

We must also be aware of how our guests view our skills. Many of our guests watch us closely because they are interested in what we are doing, therefore we must be able to do the service smoothly and skillfully. As our Technical Skill level goes up, so too does our confidence and our ability to give our attention to other important parts of the Servicing process such as home haircare and rebook.

TIME FOR ACTION!

1. **How does the level of your Technical Skills impact the quality of your guest's service experience?**

2. **Describe an extraordinary guest service experience.**

3. **Write down a Technical Skill you would like to improve.**

4. **List three ways you can improve that Technical Skill.**

    *
    *
    *

3. BALANCING GUEST CONVERSATIONS & MANAGING GUEST RELATIONSHIPS

SERVICING PART 1

There are two kinds of conversations that happen during a guest visit: social conversations and professional conversations.

SOCIAL CONVERSATIONS

Random casual conversations that involve small talk and chitchat. It's talking to our guests about what's going on with us or with them. Social conversations play a role in the servicing process by lowering tension, increasing guest rapport, and ultimately setting the stage for professional conversations.

PROFESSIONAL CONVERSATIONS

Specific conversations that revolve around the guest's look and the Big Four. These are the kinds of conversations that encourage our guests to buy more services and retail, rebook their next appointment, or send in referrals. *Top 20s are keenly aware and highly skilled at balancing social conversations with professional conversations.*

4. THE LIMITS OF TOO LITTLE SMALL TALK

Many stylists are stuck in Bottom 80 either because they are shy, afraid, or unsure of what to say and therefore say little or nothing. Or they feel it's not their job to entertain their guests with small talk. All they want is for the guest to shut up and sit still so that they can concentrate on the haircut. In both cases these stylists end up not talking about anything and miss opportunities to bond with their guests. Too little socializing limits our potential for greater income by preventing us from having professional conversations.

SHUT UP and SIT STILL!!!

5. THE DANGER OF TOO MUCH SMALL TALK

There are many different social conversations that happen every day in the salon between stylists and their guests. Many of our guests love to talk to us, they think our lives are interesting, and it seems like they want to know everything about us. Stylists stuck in Bottom 80 are more than willing to accommodate their guests by spending too much time talking about themselves. Most of these self-defeating social conversations begin when our guests ask, **"So what's new with you?"** On the right is a list of common small talk topics. **When left unchecked**, these topics can lead to small pay by turning guests off and driving the people working around us crazy from hearing it over and over again.

SMALL TALK TOPICS INCLUDE

My wedding

My husband/wife

My pregnancy

My kid's latest adventures

My new boyfriend/girlfriend

My favorite restaurant

My latest drama...

...and this is the invitation...

148

6. THE ULTIMATE HAZARD: MAKING GUESTS OUR FRIENDS

While some small talk is necessary for creating a bond with our guests, stylists caught in Bottom 80 spend way too much time socializing and too little time having conversations that relate to the services their guests are having done.

The habit of too much small talk quickly leads to the ultimate hazard, which is making guests our friends. **There is a big difference between being guest friendly and making guests our friends.** Being friendly to guests is part of the bonding process, but the moment we make a guest our friend, we feel the pressure to discount our prices or give away services for free. **Nothing condemns us to a lifetime sentence in the prison of Bottom 80 income more than the need to be liked by friends who used to be guests.**

I'm getting a deal on this...
right?

7. BREAKING UP AND REDIRECTING SMALL TALK

One of the best ways to break the habit of too little or too much small talk is by redirecting the social conversation to a professional one. **We do this by getting guests involved in what we are doing in the service process.** Involving guests in this way gets them interested and excited about how their look is evolving. When guests feel this way, they spend more money and come back more often as guests and not just as friends who expect friendly discounts and give-aways. Redirecting statements are a great way to get guests who want to spend the entire appointment socializing back on track.

REDIRECTING STATEMENTS

- *"By the way, I wanted to let you know what I'm doing with your hair to get it to..."*
- *"Let me tell you about what I'm doing here..."*
- *"Before I forget, I want to tell you about..."*

TIME FOR ACTION!

1. **On the conversation scale how would you rate your conversations with your guests?**

   VERY LITTLE SMALL TALK ←—|—|—|—|—|—|—|—|—|—|—→ A LOT OF SMALL TALK

2. **What would a balanced social and professional conversation look like to you?**

3. **How has too much or too little small talk gotten in the way of you giving your guests a great service experience?**

4. **How can you prevent yourself from talking too much about yourself?**

8. **SELLING HOME HAIRCARE PRODUCTS** | SERVICING PART 2

The Servicing Step of the Power Wheel is an excellent opportunity to have a professional conversation with our guests about using home haircare. Haircare falls into three groupings: **shampoos**, **conditioners**, and **treatments**. Conditioners can be broken down further into three categories: **rinse outs**, **leave ins**, and **treatment stylers**. Top 20s know that the right combinations of home haircare can transform hair's inner structure as well as dramatically improve its outer appearance. That's why they make teaching their guests about home haircare a part of the professional conversation during the Service experience.

9. **HOME HAIRCARE FOR COLOR GUESTS**

Because most of us find it easier to sell home haircare products to guests who color their hair, let's begin there. Checking in during a chemical service gives us an excellent opportunity to begin teaching our guests about the benefits of using our shampoos and conditioners. We do this by stressing the importance of avoiding products that fade and damage color-treated hair. We also emphasize that the hair needs to heal from the chemical processes. Some shampoos and conditioners will actually slow down that healing. Last but not least, we recommend the shampoo and conditioner that will quicken the healing process and prolong the life of the color.

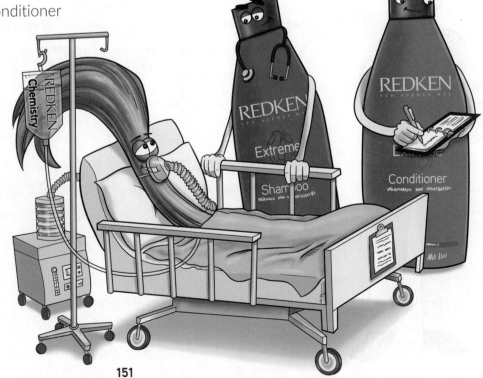

10. *OH NO!* NOT THE RETAIL RANT

I'm gonna bag up 3 of these for you right now.

The professional conversations that many stylists find the most difficult are the conversations around selling retail products. Stylists stuck in Bottom 80 hate talking to their guests about buying retail products. They believe that selling retail has nothing to do with becoming successful, and that asking guests to buy retail products isn't why they became a stylist. They say things like:

- *"I hate selling retail. It makes me feel sleezy."*
- *"I'm not going to sell that crap to my guests."*
- *"My guests don't want me to talk about that crap."*
- *"If I wanted to sell that crap I'd be working at a cosmetics counter!"*
- *"I'm not a sales person, I'm creative."*

11. STOP SELLING & START TEACHING

I love using this because...

The single biggest reason stylists stuck in Bottom 80 hate selling retail is because they believe that the act of offering retail to their guests makes them look pushy, sleazy, and manipulative.

They are totally unaware of an important fact. It's not the act of selling retail that makes us feel like we're high-pressure, manipulative salespeople, it's our intention for offering retail that makes the difference. If our intention is to sell products to our guests at their loss and our gain, then we are indeed high-pressure salespeople.

However (and this is an important however), a Top 20's intention is to TEACH guests how to make their look work for them when they style their hair at home. They believe that the products they use are liquid tools a guest *needs* and the act of offering retail is an act of *teaching* and *serving*, not of pushing and selling. We are serving the greater good of our guests, and that is an honorable act.

12. FEATURES & BENEFITS

Guests buy products not because of what the product is, but because of what the product does. When we talk too much about what the product is or what's in the product, our guests get a sense that they are being "sold." And guests hate being "sold." However, they do love to "buy." The secret to getting guests to buy home haircare products is to start talking about what the product does to help them get the looks they want.

When we talk about what a product is or what's in a product, we are talking about its **Features**. When we talk about what a product does or means for the guest, we are talking about the **Benefits** of that product.

Whenever we are teaching our guests about home haircare products, we should focus 20% of our attention on describing the Features and 80% of our attention on teaching guests about the Benefits.

FEATURES: 20%

BENEFITS: 80%

FEATURE: *What it IS*	BENEFIT: *What it DOES*	SCRIPT BUILDERS: *What to SAY*
SHAMPOO with Micro-Net, UVA & UVB Filters, Cranberry Oil, and Ceramide.	Gently cleanses, provides anti-fade protection, and maximizes vibrancy. Leaves hair strong, shiny, and manageable.	*"I love this shampoo and conditioner. It's made such a difference for so many of my guests who color their hair. It keeps their hair strong and in great shape. I never worry about their color fading."*
CONDITIONER with Apricot Oil, Glucosamine, and Glycerin.	Helps restore moisture without weighing it down. Leaves hair replenished, light, and shiny.	
PROFESSIONAL TREATMENTS with Camelina, Avocado Oil, and Olive Oil.	Custom formulas that address common hair needs like strength, moisture, color protection, softness, frizz control, and repair.	*"One of the services I have always wanted to do for you is a custom treatment. I offer it to my guests like you who need to bring more strength and moisture into their hair."*

13. WORDS MAKE A DIFFERENCE

The words we use make a huge difference when we're describing the benefits of home haircare products. When we expand our language and vocabulary, it gives our guests an exciting, impressive, and memorable experience, which always brings greater prosperity into our life. It's been said that we make our world by our words. Here is a list of powerful words that promise to make our financial world better. Some words describe problems that need to be solved, while others describe positive qualities that home haircare can offer.

PROBLEM HOME HAIRCARE WORD LIST

Breakage	Frizzy
Damaged	Lifeless
Dry, brittle	Limp
Dull	Uncontrollable
Faded	Unmanageable
Fine	Unruly
Flat	Weakened

POSITIVE HOME HAIRCARE WORD LIST

Brilliant	Protection
Clarifies	Rebalances
Detangles	Replenished
Enriches	Repairs
Full-bodied	Restores
Fullness	Shine
Luxurious	Soft
Luminous	Strengthens
Manageability	Touchable
Moisturizing	Transform
Nourishes	Volume

TIME FOR ACTION!

1. How do you feel about selling home haircare products?

2. What's the difference between selling and teaching?

3. List TWO shampoos, TWO conditioners, and ONE treatment. List the PRODUCT NAME and FEATURES. Describe their BENEFITS. In the last column write a script about the benefits of the product(s) you listed.

FEATURE: What it IS	BENEFIT: What it DOES	SCRIPT: Write down how you'll present the benefits to your guest.
2 SHAMPOOS		
2 CONDITIONERS		
1 TREATMENT		

14. **THE INCREDIBLE POWER OF TOUCH**

One of the most unique aspects of our business is that our guests give us permission to physically touch them. In that unique way what we do is similar to the medical profession, Yet there's a big difference. Our guests look forward to the relaxing experience of the shampoo. But a patient will say, "You can touch me, Doc, but hurry up, touch what you've got to touch and then get out of there, because I don't like this at all!" That big difference gives us a huge advantage. We have the incredible power to make our guests feel good physically by our very touch.

15. **THE TOP 20 BIG DEAL SHAMPOO/MASSAGE**

There's no better time to use the power of our touch to relax our guests and put them in the spending spirit than during the shampoo/massage process.

The shampoo/massage process is that part of the service experience that our guests enjoy the most. In fact they say things like:

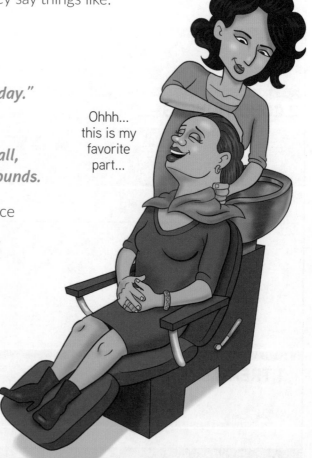

Ohhh... this is my favorite part...

- *"This is my favorite part!"*

- *"You can do this forever!"*

- *"I wish I could have this done everyday."*

- *"That feels so good!"*

- *Some guests don't say anything at all, but they make the most amazing sounds.*

Top 20s are keenly aware of the importance of the shampoo and conditioning process, and are highly skilled at making a big deal of giving a great shampoo/massage.

16. THE BOTTOM 80 HOSER HABIT

Stylists caught in Bottom 80 might save a couple of minutes by doing a quick shampoo but, in the end, lose a lot of guests and money by not giving a big deal shampoo/massage.

Avoid falling into the "Bottom 80 Hoser Habit" of thinking the shampoo/conditioning process is no big deal. If we get into the habit of rushing through the process, we end up ruining the guest's experience.

SYMPTOMS OF A BOTTOM 80 HOSER

- *Hosing the guest down with water pressure so intense that it would peel paint.*

- *Back washing the guests clothes from reckless rinsing.*

- *Giving the guest two choices of water temperature: Ice Cold or Scalding Hot!*

- *Kung Fu Masters of the 20-second shampoo.*

17. RETAIL AT THE SHAMPOO BOWL

For years many of us have been trained to talk to our guests about the products we're using as we wash and condition their hair at the shampoo bowl. If this method is working to help you sell retail products, by all means keep up the good work. But for those of us who have found that this method has stopped working, we suggest saving the home haircare conversation for the middle of the haircut or color service and allowing the guest to enjoy the experience of a big deal shampoo/massage. Many guests have heard the "product pitch" at the shampoo bowls so many times that they are now numb to it. Talking about home haircare in the middle of the service is a great place to begin a new approach.

GETTING THE HOME HAIRCARE CONVERSATION STARTED FOR *HAIRCOLOR* GUESTS

1 Check in on guests halfway through the color process and reassure them.

EXAMPLE SCRIPT: *"I'm just checking in with you to see how you're doing. Your color is coming along great and we have a few minutes left before we rinse it off."*

2 Begin teaching guests how to take care of their color at home.

EXAMPLE SCRIPT: *"By the way, make sure that over the next few days you pay close attention to what you're using to shampoo and condition your hair. It's important that what you're using is healing your hair and prolonging your color."*

3 As they respond favorably or ask what they should be using, teach them about your shampoos and conditioners for color treated hair.

EXAMPLE SCRIPT: *"Avoid using anything that will damage your hair or cause fading of your color. That's why I love what I use..."*

GETTING THE HOME HAIRCARE CONVERSATION STARTED FOR *HAIRCUT* GUESTS

1 The home haircare discussion with our haircut guests is important because these products have the power to strengthen the hair's inner structure and dramatically improve the outer appearance.

EXAMPLE SCRIPTS: *"I really like how this haircut is starting to come together, it's looking great."*

"By the way, start paying closer attention to what you're using to shampoo and condition your hair. What we use on our hair makes a much bigger difference in getting our look right everyday than most people think."

"Make sure that whatever you're using is doing the most to support your great look. Does that make sense?"

18. HOME HAIRCARE RECOMMENDATIONS

If we involve our guests during the Servicing process by talking to them about what we are doing and the results we are trying to achieve, there is a greater chance that they will become more interested in our suggestions and recommendations. They will say things like, *"What do you think I should be using on my hair?"* This is a direct invitation to give our recommendation on the shampoos and conditioners we carry, especially for color-treated hair. Whether their hair needs moisture, volume, softness, control, or strength and repair, there is a wide range of state-of-the-art products to fill those needs.

EXAMPLE SCRIPT: *"In any given month I do 40-45 color services, and here is what I use that supports the color. Many of my guests use this and love how it protects their color, so I would recommend..."*

ASKING GUESTS TO BUY HOME HAIRCARE

The easiest and safest way to ask guests if they would like to try the Home Haircare products we're suggesting is by using the S.A.N.S. approach; Smile–Ask–Nod–Shut Up.

S **S**MILE AS YOU ASK THE QUESTION.

A **A**SK THE QUESTION. *"Would you like to get started on the shampoo and conditioner we used today?"*

N **N**OD YOUR HEAD GENTLY AS YOU ASK THE QUESTION.

S **S**HUT UP. Don't say anything more. Let the guest talk.

19. NEVER BELITTLE A GUEST'S CHOICE

Some guests tell us they're using an over-the-counter product that they get at the grocery store. What they usually say is, "I've been using _____ and I like what it does." Comments like that can trigger a judgmental, sarcastic response in some of us, and we end up blurting out comments about that product at the risk of offending our guests. *"You're not using that crap are you? I use that stuff to get the grease off my stove,"* or *"Really? Even my dog hates that stuff!"*

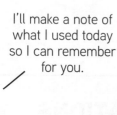

I'll make a note of what I used today so I can remember for you.

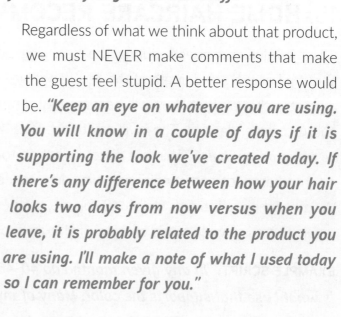

Regardless of what we think about that product, we must NEVER make comments that make the guest feel stupid. A better response would be. *"Keep an eye on whatever you are using. You will know in a couple of days if it is supporting the look we've created today. If there's any difference between how your hair looks two days from now versus when you leave, it is probably related to the product you are using. I'll make a note of what I used today so I can remember for you."*

HOME HAIRCARE SCRIPT BUILDERS

The following is a list of possible retail benefit script builders from Redken/Pureology Retail Product Guides. These are a great resource to help you find your own voice when describing retail products to your guests.

Dramatically improves your hair's appearance

Luminous shine

Adds sparkling, dimensional shine

Defends against damage

Revives hair with a bright, shiny finish

Delivers 2X more volume

Replenishes normal to dry hair

Unsurpassed haircolor protection

Guards hair against color fading caused by frequent washing

Keeps color radiant and shiny

Protects haircolor from UV damage and fading

Helps repair sun-damaged hair

Fortifies hair that is prone to breaking, splitting, or snapping off

Prevents further damage

Lasting frizz-fighting power

Intense repair

Restores hair to its youthful state

Age-correcting treatments for your hair

TIME FOR ACTION!

1. **What are your favorite shampoos and conditioners and why are they your favorites?**

2. **Use the word lists on page 154 and the script builders on this page to write a script for describing your favorite shampoo and conditioner to a guest.**

3. **What gets in your way when asking guests to purchase home haircare?**

20. TOP 20 RESPONSES TO GUEST RETAIL REACTIONS

Some guests are unsure of the value of our suggestions and their unfavorable reactions will require a graceful response. Don't get discouraged and remember—we're planting seeds for future visits. Here are some common guest reactions accompanied by graceful responses.

GUEST: *"Are you trying to sell me?"* or *"Do you get commission when you sell these products?"*

Simply turn your guest towards you, apologize, and then clarify your intentions. As soon as guests know that our purpose is to help them, they will trust us. If they think we're trying to sell them at their loss and our gain, they will shut down the process.

> **TOP 20 RESPONSE:** *"I apologize if I have offended you. My intention is to educate you on how to take care of your hair at home and maintain the look we've achieved today."*

GUEST: *"I like what I am using."* or *"I'll use up what I have."*

Never criticize your guest. When we are critical of our guests' product choices, their anxiety goes up and their trust in us drops. Guests need proof that what we're saying is true. Plant a seed and later, when they're working with their hair, they will remember our information.

> **TOP 20 RESPONSE:** *"Great, you'll know in a couple of days if what you're using now is going to make your look work for you."*

GUEST: *"Shampoo and conditioner are all pretty much the same, right?"*

Some guests are skeptical. Don't push. Instead offer proof by sharing examples of guests who have had success with your product. Doing this helps guests see the value in what we are offering. Some guests need more information when they are making decisions about spending money.

> **TOP 20 RESPONSE #1:** *"Well, just as you would be careful about how you would clean an expensive silk blouse, you want to be just as careful about what you're using to protect and prolong the new color we just put in your hair."*

TOP 20 RESPONSE #2: *"I've just treated your hair with a chemical color service. In essence, I've done surgery on your hair. I've opened up the cuticle. Be mindful of using products that are specifically designed to quickly heal and strengthen your hair."*

GUEST: *"How much is this going to cost me?"*

Some guests are price conscious. Do not assume that means "no." It means they need help feeling comfortable about spending money. Make it affordable by breaking down the price into a few cents a day. Doing this eliminates their guilt about spending money. Guests who can afford our services, can also afford the products they need to make their look work.

TOP 20 RESPONSE: *"I appreciate your concern about the cost. What's great about this product is it works so well that you only need a small amount. It ends up costing you only a few cents a day."*

GUEST: *"I can buy it cheaper down the street."*

Some guests are misinformed about buying our products for less money in other stores. Once guests understand the direct benefit to them in getting products from our salon, they're more likely to spend their money with us. Our purpose here is to give them a great reason to buy products from us.

TOP 20 RESPONSE: *"My hope is that you would buy it from me. Most of the proceeds we get from guests who buy products from our salon fund our education. A couple times a year I go to advanced training to learn the latest trends so that when I return I have new ideas to offer you."*

Top 20 Stylists know that being well trained in product knowledge is essential to building a Top 20 Clientele. As a result they sell more home haircare products, retain more guests, and earn substantially more money.

KEY ELEMENTS OF

HOME HAIRCARE

Top 20s are keenly aware and highly skilled in making sure the service they're providing is what the guest wants. A Top 20 Service is made of the following elements.

☐ **CONTINUE IMPROVING TECHNICAL SKILLS:** Never before has having a deeper understanding and wider range of technical skills in all of the following areas been so critical to our greater financial success.

- **CUT & DESIGN:** Practicing new looks and new techniques.

- **COLOR:** Learning about the pre-treatments, developers, lighteners, permanent and demi-permanent colors, glossings, mixing, and processing.

- **TEXTURE & STRAIGHTENING:** Understanding different kinds of permanent waves and the results they produce; straighteners and how to use them safely.

- **TOOLS:** Having and being able to use scissors, clippers, combs, razors, bowls, brushes, and applicators.

☐ **CLEAN & ORDERLY STATION:** Guests sitting in our chair have a clear view of our station. Having a clean, orderly station sends a message to our guests that we are organized, competent, and can be trusted to take good care of them.

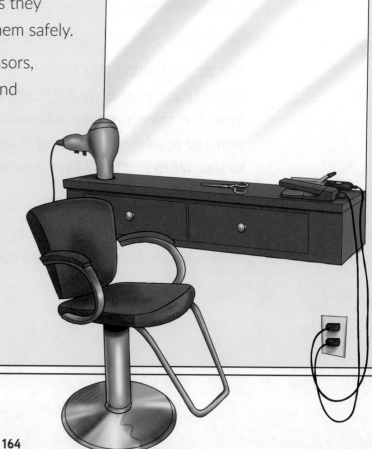

SERVICING

HOME HAIRCARE

☐ **BALANCE SOCIAL AND PROFESSIONAL CONVERSATIONS:** There are two kinds of conversations that happen during a guest visit: Social Conversation and Professional Conversation. Social Conversations play a role in the servicing process by lowering tension and increasing guest rapport, while Professional Conversations encourage our guests to buy more services and retail, rebook their next appointment, or send in referrals. Use the redirecting technique when the conversation has become too social. *"By the way I wanted to let you know what I'm doing with your hair to get it to..."* or, *"Something just occurred to me as I was cutting your hair..."*

☐ **TEACH GUESTS ABOUT HOME HAIRCARE:** Checking in during a chemical service gives us an excellent opportunity to begin teaching our guests about the benefits of using our shampoos and conditioners. Check in on the guest halfway through the color process to reassure them. *"Your color is looking great and I want to make sure that over the next few days you pay close attention to what you're using to shampoo and condition your hair. It's important that what you're using is healing your hair and prolonging your color. You really want to avoid using anything that will damage your hair and strip out the color. Does that make sense?"*

☐ **BIG DEAL SHAMPOO/MASSAGE:** The shampoo/massage process is that part of the service experience that our guests enjoy the most. Top 20s are keenly aware of the importance of the shampoo and conditioning process and are highly skilled at making a big deal of giving a great shampoo/massage.

STEPS FOR SELLING HOME HAIRCARE PRODUCTS

STEP 1	**BEGIN BY CHECKING IN WITH GUEST**

Checking in helps to reassure our guests that everything is going as planned. *"I'm checking your color and it is looking great. We have a few minutes left before we rinse it off."*

STEP 2	**EDUCATE GUEST ON THE IMPORTANCE OF HOME HAIRCARE**

Because we want our guests' haircolor to heal and stay fresh and vibrant, it's important for us to educate them on how to take care of it. *"By the way, start paying closer attention to what you're using to shampoo and condition your hair. What we use on our hair makes a much bigger difference in getting our look right everyday than most people think. I just want to make sure that whatever you're using is doing the most to support your great look. Does that make sense?"*

STEP 3	**HOME HAIRCARE PRODUCT RECOMMENDATIONS**

Oftentimes a guest has a favorable response and will ask us what we think they should be using. At this time you would make a shampoo and conditioner recommendation. *"Every day I depend on this product to protect and strengthen my guests' hair after I've colored it. That's why I recommend..."*

STEP 4	**ASK FOR THE COMMITMENT AND HANDLE GUEST RESISTANCE OR REACTIONS WHEN NECESSARY**

If guests have less-than-favorable reactions to our home haircare presentation, respond gracefully. *"I apologize if I have offended you. My intention is to educate you on how to take care of your hair at home and maintain the look we've achieved today."*

STEP 5	**ASK FOR THE COMMITMENT**

Use the S.A.N.S. approach.
S: Smile.
A: Ask the question. *"Would you like to get started on the shampoo and conditioner we used today?"*
N: Nod.
S: Shut up.

21. THE PROFESSIONAL CONVERSATION FOR REBOOKING GUESTS

The single most important action that drives up our REPEAT business is our ability to rebook our guests for their next visit. The Servicing step of the Power Wheel provides an excellent opportunity to have a professional conversation with our guests about reserving their next appointment.

Rebooking is a Top 20 success strategy because guests who rebook with us:

- *Give us 2–3 more visits per year than guests who don't.*
- *Enable us to earn much greater income because they return more frequently.*
- *Create a more predictable financial future for us and eliminate financial uncertainty.*
- *Allow us to continue evolving their look by planning the services and products we will offer them during their next visit.*
- *Buy more chemical services, additional services, and products.*
- *Send in more referrals who are more likely to rebook with us.*

The bottom line is that rebooking empowers us to make a lot more money by building an awesome repeat clientele in the fastest period of time!

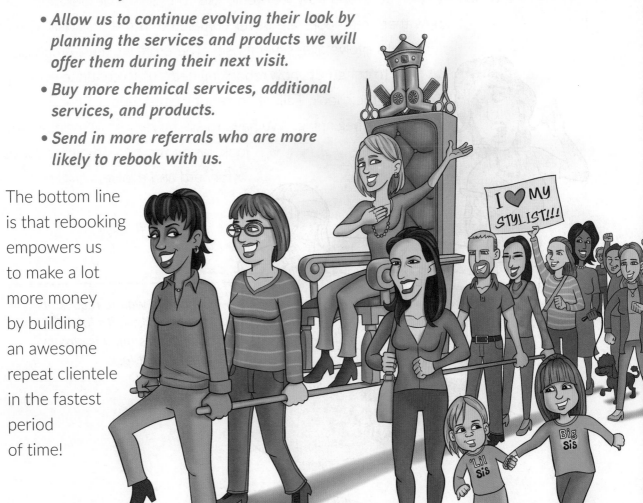

22. **TIMING IS EVERYTHING**

Traditionally, asking guests to rebook always happened at the front desk when the service was finished. It sounded something like this: *"Would you like to reserve your next appointment?"* At that point the guest's typical response is, *"No that's OK. I'll just call."*

The disadvantage of waiting until the end to ask about rebooking is that for most guests the appointment is over and their attention has moved on to what they need to do next. **"I've got to get back to work"** or **"I've got to pick up the kids"** or **"What am I going to make for supper?"**

When we reconsider the timing of a rebook conversation, we realize that there is a better option with a much higher success rate. That time is in the middle of the service process. This is a time when we are able to talk to our guests about the look we're creating and how we would like to evolve that look. Top 20s know that great looks are never completed in the first visit. Great looks evolve over several visits. Therefore we must emphasize to our guests how rebooking helps us to continue evolving their look. Failure to rebook puts us both back at the beginning. We have to start over just to maintain the look, losing the opportunity to move forward and evolve.

When we wait to rebook at the front desk, it's too late. Our guest's mind is already on the next task.

GETTING THE REBOOK CONVERSATION STARTED FOR *HAIRCOLOR* GUESTS

When getting the rebooking conversation started it's important to remember that the term "rebooking" is what we use for tracking purposes. The better word to use with our guest is RESERVATION or RESERVE. So we ask our guest to RESERVE their next appointment with us, we don't use the term rebook.

1 Check in on guests halfway through the color process. Reassure them that their color is coming along great.

EXAMPLE SCRIPT: *"I'm checking your color and it is looking great. We have a few minutes left before we rinse it off."*

2 Begin teaching guests how to keep their look evolving by reserving their next visit now.

EXAMPLE SCRIPT: *"I'm excited about the look that we are working on for you, and it would be great if I could see you in five weeks. That way we can keep your look moving forward."*

3 Have your calendar ready to zero in on dates for their next appointment.

EXAMPLE SCRIPT: *"That would be the third week of October. Is there a day of that week that works for you to make a reservation?"*

GETTING THE REBOOK CONVERSATION STARTED...

...FOR *HAIRCUT* GUESTS

Oftentimes as we start working with our guests' hair, new ideas to enhance their look will naturally come to us. These ideas can become conversation pieces that show guests the depth of our creativity and give them something to look forward to on their next visit.

Reassure guests that their haircut is coming along great and that you are looking forward to evolving their look on their next visit.

EXAMPLE SCRIPT: *"I really like how this haircut is taking shape and it would be great if I could see you in five weeks. That way we can keep your look moving forward. That would be the third week of March. Is there a day of that week that works for you to reserve a time?"*

...FOR *RELAXER* GUESTS

Our guests who are having their hair relaxed need multiple reservations for their touch-up relaxer as well as reservations for maintenance in between relaxing.

Reassure guests that their relaxer is coming along great and that you want to be able to maintain their look.

EXAMPLE SCRIPT: *"It would be great to see you in four weeks for your relaxer touch-up and then next Wednesday for your in-between maintenance reservation. What time on Wednesday works for you to reserve a time?"*

23. **FEAR OF "NO"**

One of the most common mistakes that some stylists make is waiting to see if a new guest returns for a second or third visit before asking them if they want to rebook. Stylists who are stuck in Bottom 80 say that they are afraid to ask new guests to reserve their next appointment because:

- *Before asking new guests to rebook, I always wait for them to come back to see me first. That way I know that they really like me and are pleased with what I do.*

- *If I do ask the guest to rebook and they say "no," that means they don't like what I've done and for sure they don't like me, and I hate it when that happens!*

- *Asking on the first visit is just too risky because I'm not sure they like me and I don't want to be rejected.*

Top 20s know that the fastest way to build a strong, repeat clientele is by getting new guests to rebook. They do this by **Bonding**, **Consulting**, and **Servicing** new guests in ways that create an extraordinary experience. Guests then look forward to coming back and are happy to reserve their next appointment.

BOTTOM 80 REBOOKING BLUNDERS

"Did you want to reserve your next appointment?...	*...or wait to call me?"*
"Would you like to reserve your next appointment?...	*...or no?"*
"Would you like to pick a date to make your next reservation?...	*...or do you want to think about it?"*

24. **TOP 20 RESPONSES TO GUEST REBOOK REACTIONS**

There will be some guests who are resistant to rebooking. Don't get discouraged by this. Respond gracefully, and remember that once again we're planting seeds and those seeds will take root. Here's a common guest reaction and a suggestion on how to gracefully respond to it.

GUEST: *"I don't have my calendar with me, so I don't know what I have open. I'll just call you."*

TOP 20 RESPONSE: *"No problem. Let's reserve a time that you think will work and put it down now. If you find that it doesn't work, just give me a call and we'll find a time that does. If we wait too long, I won't be available because I'm booking up quickly."*

TIME FOR ACTION!

1. **What would help you feel more confident when you ask guests to reserve their next appointment?**

2. **What does 2–3 more visits from our guests per year mean for you financially?**

3. **How would asking for the reservation during the service change your guest's response and increase your success at rebooking?**

KEY ELEMENTS OF TOP 20 SERVICING

REBOOKING

☐ **REBOOKING AND THE BIG FOUR**

The third part of the Big Four is called Repeat, and rebooking is one of the main activities of building a strong, repeat clientele. Having a solid base of repeat guests is essential to developing the right combination of the Big 4. As our base of repeats grows, we have more guests to sell our services and retail to, as well as more guests to get referrals from.

☐ **REBOOKING AND THE EVOLVING LOOK**

Top 20s are keenly aware of the importance of creating looks that evolve over several visits. Working this way gives our guests something to look forward to and a reason to rebook their next visit before leaving the salon.

Getting our guests to rebook their next visit within a 4–6 week window of time is a must for keeping their look fresh, evolving, and up-to-date.

"If you are happy with your look, you're going to really love what we do on your next visit, because I can build on what I did today."

☐ **TIMING THE REBOOK**

A great time to ask guests to rebook is in the middle of the service process. There is a much higher success rate at getting the guest to rebook when we ask during the service process instead of waiting until the end of the appointment.

 # SERVICE STOMPERS

AUTOMATIC PILOT

Instead of giving the guest an extraordinary service experience with home haircare and rebook offerings, we go on automatic pilot and do hair in our sleep. At best the service is ordinary. At worst, it's sub-standard.

MESSY MISSY

Servicing guests in a messy, grubby, and disorganized manner. Having no regard for water or color dripping down the guest's face, neck, and back, causing the guest to feel frustrated, annoyed, and embarrassed.

DESERTER

Carelessly deserting color service guests who may fret and worry. Meanwhile the deserter leaves to eat, smoke, rest, and complain. All the while a nervous guest sits with chemical solution dripping, burning, and wondering, *"Where the heck is my hairdresser? My scalp's on fire!"*

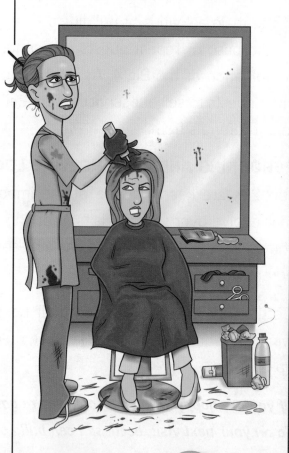

CHATTER BOX

Compulsive talkers who spend the entire appointment talking, talking, and more talking about themselves, their drama, and all their stuff. As a result they never get around to talking about the guest's look.

The following are common examples of how we stomp opportunities for greater income when we fall into Bottom 80 Servicing.

LOW CHARGE-NO CHARGE

Making friends with their guests and then keeping their new friends happy by giving them free services and/or charging them lower prices.

AVOIDER

Avoiding any conversations that involve selling home haircare products and rebooking their guests because doing that makes for a pushy salesperson and "I'll die broke before I let that happen!"

X-RAY VISION

Using super powers to look into their guests' purses and decide who can afford the very expensive retail products the salon sells. Always concluding, "I'm not going to try selling these expensive products to my guests. They're like me, they don't have that kind of money!"

TIME FOR ACTION!

1. **Identify those Service Stompers you can relate to most.**

2. **How has that Stomper held you back from giving your guests an extraordinary service experience and enjoying greater income?**

STEPS FOR REBOOKING GUESTS

STEP 1

BEGIN BY CHECKING IN WITH THE GUEST

Checking in helps to reassure our guest that everything is going as planned.

CHECK-IN SCRIPT FOR COLOR: *"I'm checking your color and it is looking great. We have a few minutes left before we rinse it off."*

CHECK-IN SCRIPT FOR HAIRCUTS: *"As I was working with your hair, I just had a great idea about how we could evolve your look."*

STEP 2

PRESENT RESERVATION

Make sure you have your calendar ready as you are presenting and looking for dates for the reservation. Make sure you use the term RESERVATION or RESERVE instead of pre-book or rebook when speaking to the guest.

REBOOK SCRIPT FOR COLOR: *"I'm excited about the look that we are working on for you. It would be great if I could see you in five weeks. That way we can keep your look moving forward. That would be the third week of October. Is there a day of that week that works for you to make a reservation?"*

REBOOK SCRIPT FOR HAIRCUTS: *"It would be great if I could see you in five weeks. That would be the third week of October. Is there a day of that week that works for you to reserve a time?"*

STEP 3

HANDLE GUEST RESISTANCE OR REACTIONS WHEN NECESSARY

Gracefully handle guests who are unsure about rebooking.

REBOOK SCRIPT FOR REACTIONS: *"No problem. Let's find a day and a time that you think will work and reserve it. If you find that it doesn't work, just give me a call and we'll find a time that does. If we wait too long to reserve, I won't be available at a time that works for you because I'm booking up quickly."*

SERVICING SUMMARY

Servicing is the third step of the Power Wheel and it's all about giving an extraordinary experience to each and every guest who sits in our chair. The Servicing step is made up of many parts: balancing Social and Professional Conversations, performing the service effectively, teaching guests about home haircare products, and rebooking repeat visits to keep their look evolving.

The positive feelings that a guest gets from being served in this way lead to higher service and retail sales and the ability to build a repeat clientele in record time. Remember it's about being guest-friendly without making guests your friends. **Building a great clientele demands that we become highly skilled at Top 20 Servicing—all of which leads to an income beyond our wildest dreams.**

FINDING PAST OPPORTUNITIES

STEP 1

Go back 1 month and look in your book for missed SERVICE opportunities that would have increased your AVERAGE DOLLAR PER DAY and AVERAGE DOLLAR PER GUEST.

- Charging lower prices to repeat guests (friends) than "new."
- Giving away free services.
- Not making the service offering (or talking guests out of it).

How much service money did you come up with?

STEP 2

Go back 1 month and look in your book for missed RETAIL opportunities that would have increased your RETAIL TO SERVICE number.

- Assuming certain guests can't afford it.
- Not sharing the Features and Benefits of home haircare.
- Forgetting to ask.

How much retail money did you come up with?

SIX KEYS TO CRUCIAL CONVERSATIONS

1. Top 20 Attitude: Cool, Calm, and Collected
2. Plan this conversation for the end of the appointment
3. Accept Responsibility
4. Apologize
5. OPOs/OPJs (Other People's Opinions & Judgments) are none of your business
6. Let it go and move on...

"Nothing condemns us to a life sentence in the prison of Bottom 80 income more than the need to be liked by friends who used to be guests."

I'm getting a deal on this... right?

CREATE YOUR HOME HAIRCARE PRESENTATION

Use the STEPS FOR SELLING HOME HAIRCARE PRODUCTS (PAGE 166)
to write your own scripts.

1: CHECKING IN WITH GUEST

- *Make eye contact and smile.*
- *Reassure guest that everything is going as planned.*

Write your reassuring statement for a haircolor guest:

_____

_____

_____

2: EDUCATE ON THE IMPORTANCE OF HOME HAIRCARE

Write your teaching script here:

_____

_____

_____

_____

_____

3: HOME HAIRCARE RECOMMENDATIONS

- *Choose a shampoo and conditioner for haircolor guests and for haircut-only guests.*

Write your home haircare recommendations for <u>HAIRCOLOR</u> guests:

_____

_____

_____

Write your home haircare recommendations for <u>HAIRCUT</u> guests:

_____

_____

_____

CREATE YOUR REBOOK PRESENTATION

Use the STEPS FOR REBOOKING GUESTS (PAGE 176) *to write your own scripts.*

1: CHECKING IN WITH GUEST

• *Make eye contact and smile.*
• *Reassure guest that everything is going as planned.*

This could be the same reassuring statement used for your home haircare presentation:

_____

_____

_____

_____

_____

_____

2: REBOOK PRESENTATION

• *Make sure you have a calendar available.*

Write your script for making a rebook presentation. Remember to use the terms "reservation" or "reserve," NOT rebook or pre-book.

_____

_____

_____

_____

_____

_____

_____

_____

_____